BUS AMERICA

REVELATION OF A REDNECK

BUS AMERICA

REVELATION OF A REDNECK

BY

QUAY HANNA

COVER DESIGNED AND CREATED BY

MICHAEL EVANKO AND NATE KRESGE

MIDDLE RELIEF PUBLISHING
MILLERSVILLE, PA

This second edition is dedicated to my wife and son,
Shannon and Quay, Jr.

Preface to 2nd Edition

I know most of the time people skip the preface, but you really need to read this. A lot has changed since the first edition of *Bus America: Revelation of a Redneck*.

When I took this bus trip I was twenty-three years old, freshly graduated from college, and bitter at the world. As I traveled, I realized the significance of my life and nothing has been the same since. A life of self examination has been so much better for me than just trudging through the daily routine that I wanted to share my experience with those who may never have the opportunity to take such a trip. That's why I wrote this book.

When I published my tome in 1997, I didn't think much would happen. Maybe I would sell a few to friends and family members, but then I would have to decide what to do with the remaining 1,047 copies of the book that would haunt my closet. I never believed it would be necessary to write a preface to the second edition. But here I sit, almost nine years later, trying to explain things I never thought I would have to explain.

Soon after the book's publication, local schools invited me to speak about my life-changing experiences. Each time I spoke, I remembered the countless boring guest speakers we had in high school and I strived to not become one. I attempted many an outrageous way to make my point, and it seemed to work. Young people responded well, and I found myself doing full assemblies in auditoriums, as well as acting as a professional consultant in schools suffering racial difficulties. In the past nine years, I've done over 800 presentations around the country and have helped more than a dozen schools recover from full blown racial crises. Not bad for a hick from Strasburg, Pennsylvania, huh?

My career certainly hasn't been without criticism. The difficulty with a topic like racism is that no matter what you say, someone will be be offended. Most people, however, see that my passion is genuine, and that my objectives are simple - love your neighbor as yourself, think before you speak and act, reflect on another's position before determining your own. When we think about our lives, we are more likely to think about the lives of others.

I have been criticized for some of the things you are going to read in this book: the way I often referred to women, the constant cracks against overweight people, the derogatory way I judged many bus riders. Please remember, I was twenty-three years old when I began this journey. I was seeing America for the first time. I didn't correct all my flaws during the nine weeks of this trip, but God certainly began a new work in my life by changing my views about other races. He continues to shape and mold these views to His will. But I felt it prudent to give an accurate portrayal of who I was when I left my hometown, during the journey, and at the end of the journey.

Another difference in this edition is that the profanity has been replaced with the innocuous "!@#$%&." For those of you that find this cheesy, that's OK. I do, too. But I am a speaker in public schools and market to school libraries, I don't want taxpayers to get the wrong idea about my objectives. If profanity in this book keeps me from sharing my message, it is not worth it. Besides, the symbols allow you to substitute as mild or as foul a word as you want. Knock yourself out!

I want to thank the many people who supported me since the beginning and who have stuck with me through this second edition. I am one of the few people in the world who can say they love their jobs, and would choose it again if given the opportunity. That's all I ever wanted to accomplish.

Table of Contents

Introduction

Why the bus?

Good question. Any knowledge or study of bus riding in America reveals that it is certainly not an ideal mode of transportation. Bus riding is inefficient. It can be extremely slow and transfers have to be made at ridiculous hours of the morning. It can take days to reach a location by bus that would normally only require hours by car.

There are cramped quarters on the bus and riders are often sweaty and smelly. People of various sizes, shapes and colors ride the bus and inevitably you will have some sort of contact with them.

So why would a twenty-three year old from Strasburg, Pennsylvania take the bus across America? I chose the bus, not because of the advantages or disadvantages it offered in travel, but simply because it allowed me to travel. My parents were from the small town of Strasburg, Pennsylvania. My grandparents were from the small town of Strasburg, Pennsylvania. My great-grandparents were from the small town of Strasburg, Pennsylvania. Strasburg is not a bad place, but isn't there something more to America?

I believed the journey across the United States would be the only way to experience this country for what it really is; something bigger than Strasburg and something bigger than Pennsylvania. I wanted to know America: see it, touch it, taste it, and experience it for all her grandeur and ugliness. I was tired of reading about it, tired of watching it in the movies and on television. I needed to experience it for myself.

Bus travel has many deficiencies, but so did I. Bus travel helped me begin to deal with my shortcomings and to make changes that have made my life better. I have begun to learn about my purpose in life and how to act upon it daily. When we begin living because we see a reason behind life, we begin to love others in their attempt to live life as well. It is my hope that within these pages you will begin to think about your own purpose in life. You've only got one, so don't waste it.

This is one man's story about a life altering trip across America. Won't you join me for the ride?

1

It was overcast that morning. I was shoving the last of my stuff into a duffel bag when Dad came into my room. "Are you sure you want to do this?" he said, with a look of sadness in his eyes.

"Yes. I'm sure!" I shot back.

I wasn't angry, but I was sick of hearing the question from everyone. It didn't take much to get my blood boiling.

Dad left it at that.

I continued stuffing as I glared in his direction, but to be honest, I wasn't sure.

I was born in Buck, Pennsylvania. That's an awesome name for a hick town, don't you think? I lived there for the first five years of my life. My parents were forced to move as the house we rented was being sold. With few choices, my dad moved us back to a section of the county where he had grown up.

The Hanna farm was located about six miles outside the little town of Strasburg, nestled right in the heart of God's country, Lancaster County, Pennsylvania. My dad's mom died when he was three and with his drunk of a father unable to care for him, our relatives on a farm down the road raised him. My parents' house sat on the corner of this original Hanna farm. The majority of the acreage was still fields and woods, only now the Amish cared for it instead of my family.

These were my roots. This is where the Hannas came from Ireland to settle. This is where my great uncles ran moonshine during prohibition. This is where other families like mine had lived for generations on their farms. The Rudys. The Wimers. The Drucks. These families had always seemed to live here. These farms, big and small, were broken up only by the occasional house, a second rate campground, and a trailer park known as the place to purchase drugs. This was my home. These were my people.

But I wasn't exactly like the Hannas that had come before me. I was the first to graduate high school with an "A" average. I was the first to speak at my high school commencement ceremony. I was the first to graduate from college. My family considered me smart, and although I was good at working with my hands, the family held high hopes that I would be the one to break the chain of blue collar work done by the Hannas since the beginning of our existence.

My dad, who was a truck washer for UPS, once told me, "Quay, I want you to get a college degree. I want you to do something other than physical labor for your job. I want you to use your brain. You have to understand, I'm just tired all the time, and I don't want you to have to live life that way."

That's why he sounded so disappointed that day in my room while I was packing. Here I was with a degree in English, and instead of going out and getting a "real" job, I had just spent the six months since graduation working construction. Now, I was preparing to take a two month bus trip across America. I knew what he wanted me to do. I knew what everyone was telling me to do. I knew what was the logical thing to do. I also knew I couldn't do it.

Sometimes we bombard young people with so much talk about life and careers, that it makes the journey into adulthood sound miserable. I chastise grownups who tell teenagers that this is the "best time of their lives." They're only sixteen years old, and this is the best time of their lives? Does that mean the next seventy years are going to suck? At twenty-three, that scared me. I didn't want to reach middle age and realize my life was merely a daily struggle to survive.

For a majority of America, however, that is reality. There are few people who can say they love their job and enjoy their life. I don't criticize them for doing what is necessary to support their families. In fact, I have a lot of respect for them.

I'm talking about something different. I was twenty-three

years old at the time I began my trip. I had already paid off my debt for college. I was not collecting welfare, unemployment, or food stamps. I was not married, I had no children, and I was unemployed for the winter. I didn't know what I wanted to "do" with my life, so I decided to see America. I thought this trip might teach me some things. I thought it might point me in a "career direction." All I knew for sure, though, was that it wasn't going to be boring.

My bag was packed and I waited on the couch for my parents to gather their things. They were in the parental stall, those methodical, confusing moments when they try and take enough time so that their idiot children can get their acts together and wise up. It wasn't going to work with this idiot.

"Let's go! Let's go!" I encouraged.

"Just hold on. Your father has to find a hat."

My father has hundreds of hats, mostly from local stores that give them away to loyal customers. He usually only wore about two or three of them, though. I grabbed the J.B. Zimmerman Hardware hat and threw it to him. He plopped it on his balding head.

We crammed ourselves into the little 1982 Chevette, and faded into the fog of that dreary Thursday morning. I had lied about my departure time anticipating the parental stall and not wanting to somehow be "conveniently" late. We arrived at the station well ahead of time. Dad parked and turned off the car.

We sat in the quiet of the bus station parking lot, not talking or even glancing at one another. Looking back, I guess I don't know what I would have said as a parent either. "Good job wasting your money on college?" "When did you become so stupid?" "Don't get killed?"

I had hoped that it wouldn't come to this. I just wanted to be alone and get started on this adventure. I wished they hadn't even turned off the car, but instead slowed down just enough so that I could jump out of it and yell, "See you later!" But it looked like they wanted to stay until the bus arrived. I also didn't want mom getting involved in some long, drawn out cry at the station. They were my parents and I loved them, but I had to do this without them.

"Uh, look," I started as delicately as possible, "I was hoping to spend some time alone before I left. You know, to get my thoughts together and write in my journal. Nothing personal."

I looked at Mom and thought, "Oh no. Here it comes."

Instead her reply was, "OK. See you honey. Be careful."

"Take care, son," Dad added.

And with that the little four cylinder fired up and they were gone. I stood in the rain, alone in the parking lot. I felt like I was going to have a long, drawn out cry.

I took a good, hard look around. You have to understand. The Lancaster Greyhound station is in the heart of Lancaster city. It isn't a big city, but it has plenty of big city problems. In fact, I hated the city. It was dirty and run down. I was always reading about some drug deal gone bad or someone getting knifed downtown. It made me wonder why anyone would want to visit let alone live there. Besides, there were way too many blacks and Puerto Ricans around. I liked my areas nice and white. It seemed that every place these people inhabited was dirty, dangerous, or disgusting.

I stood in the parking lot realizing I was out of my element. This small town country boy wasn't welcome here, and I had only ventured in to catch the bus. I hoped these people would understand that.

I entered the station. The building was old and musty. There were wooden benches scattered throughout the place, and the attendant stood behind a barred window. I wasn't sure what to do, so I stood there for a bit, trying to look like I knew what I was doing. Finally, the guy behind the counter said, "Well, what do you want?"

"I'll take a one way ticket to Atlanta."

It felt good saying that, but at the same time a bit odd. Asking for a one way ticket indicated that I wasn't coming back the same way I was going. That was scary. Even scarier was the fact that I was going to Atlanta, a big city that only existed in my mind. The reason I decided to make Atlanta my first destination was because a good friend of mine in the Army was stationed there, and asked me to visit him during my trip.

I wished he were stationed someplace more accessible. Atlanta? There were surely going to be people there that hated me. I would probably be the only white person around, and I figured I would be jumped the second I stepped off that bus. But I had to go. I just had to.

The attendant said it would take approximately seventeen hours to get to Atlanta, and that I was to take my duffel bag to get tagged for baggage or carry it with me. I opted for the latter.

I sat on one of the benches and looked around the empty station. It was deathly silent in the room, without even the faintest sound of the usual cheesy music one hears in a waiting area like this one. I had butterflies that felt more like nausea than adrenaline. I sat there, looking straight ahead. Maybe I should write something down. Maybe I should walk around. Maybe I should just return my ticket, call mom and dad, and just. . . I don't know.

The silence was abruptly interrupted when a Spanish girl burst into the station, pushing the door so hard that it banged against the wall. She rushed across the building, headed straight towards me.

I thought, "Ah, #!@*&! It's already happening! Word had spread throughout the city that some hick had the nerve to set foot on their turf, and they sent this girl to take me out!"

I pulled my stuff near me, put on my meanest face, and was ready to take whatever she was giving.

Suddenly she shouted, "Yo, when the #!@*& does the bus for New York leave?!"

Her words blew past my ears in the direction of the attendant.

"Five minutes ago," he said without looking up from his magazine.

"Son-of-a-#!@*&! What the #!@*&! This is such #!@*&! Yous are all a pain in the #!@*& !" This went on for a few moments, but the attendant didn't say a word.

Suddenly, she looked directly at me.

Oh, no! Here it comes! I figured she'd say something like, "What are you looking at Cracker? What's a stupid redneck like you doing in the city?"

She was dressed in the style of the day: baggy black jeans, black Doc Martens, and a hooded pullover emblazoned with the Miami Hurricanes logo. Team insignia wear always made me laugh, especially when the sports teams started gearing their styles and colors to meet the demand of people who didn't care at all about the teams. Rappers wear the stuff in their videos and suddenly it is the "in" thing, and all the city people wear the same stuff. I would have loved to ask this girl to name just one player on the Miami Hurricanes. Unfortunately, I was too busy pissing myself in fear.

"You got a quarter?" she said at me, rather than to me.

I fumbled for some change in my pocket.

"Uh . . .yeah . . .here . . ."

She took the money and without a word she was out the door, banging the wall the same way as when she entered.

The room was completely silent again. I felt completely alone. I hadn't even left Lancaster yet, and I was scared to death. I dug in my pocket for another quarter to call home. Maybe my parents would come and get me. Before I made it to the phone, though, the attendant said, "That's your bus that just pulled up."

I put the quarter away, walked over, and got on.

As I made my way back the aisle in search of a seat, one thing was painfully obvious. I was going to be the minority on this ride. It seemed all eyes were on me as I searched for the right seat in which to sit. I was afraid that if I sat in a certain place I would seem too aggressive, and if I sat in another place I would seem scared. I just didn't want to piss off any of these people. I was well educated in what they do to people like me. I finally picked a seat that was comfortably located away from the front, but not too far back.

At first I tried to get accustomed to my surroundings. It was about 5:30 p.m., and in January that meant it was already dark. The lack of light made it difficult for me to find my tickets which had fallen to the floor. I was also having trouble getting my duffel bag stuffed under my seat. I didn't want to put it in the holder above my seat for fear of forgetting it or having it stolen. All the bus folks looked at me and I felt as if they were thinking, "Stupid Rube."

I finally settled in and slowly examined my surroundings. I was feeling quite uncomfortable, and not because of the seats. As I sat there, I tried to remember any moment to that point in my life when I was a minority. I tried to think of one place where I had been surrounded by more people who were unlike me than like me. I couldn't think of any; No movie theater, no party, no convenience store, no pizza joint, no gas station, no business, no church, no supermarket, no nothing.

I guess it made sense, though. Where I was from was mostly white people. It would have been difficult for me to be a minority anywhere at home. It wasn't like I had never interacted with blacks, Hispanics, Asians, etc. My high school, though far from diverse, had a couple of minority students each year. In fact, there were two black girls there during my four years, and I was cool with them both. We had study hall together, and I would let them sit at my table. But I didn't really consider them "black." When I thought of "black," I was talking about the loud, obnoxious, type who thought he was better than me. The guy who thought I owed him something. Sometimes certain whites call these individuals the ones with "attitude."

I lived with a black guy like that my junior year in college. He was the type I would have called "black." He was into gangsta' rap (old school, like NWA), wore a lot of gold (also known as "bling" or "ice"), and hung out with lots of other blacks. They would talk about people being racist towards them, but oftentimes I thought they brought it on themselves. In fact, for as much as I now believe that interaction helps combat racism, in my case, it increased my prejudice.

I remember one of my roommate's friends who was a few years older than us. He would occasionally hang out at our place on the weekends. When he took a job near Philly, he often told us how bad and dangerous his area was. He explained it by saying, "It's a real bad neighborhood. You know what I mean? Drugs, violence, blacks, everywhere." And this guy was black! I didn't understand why people got mad at me for being a racist, since I had met more than one black who seemed to hate his own kind.

Besides, I was tired of trying. I was raised to be polite, but it seemed like the other side wasn't trying very hard. Even though I had known a few people of color, and may have even called a few of them "friends" in the course of my years, I was willing to sacrifice them to what I really felt. My mantra was, "I'm going to be a racist until I am proven wrong." I preferred people who were like me: good, old-fashioned, hard working country boys, who knew that to keep it white was to keep it right.

I discovered early on during the trip that most buses do not go directly to their destinations. On the first leg of this trip I was headed to Atlanta, but I had to change buses in York, Pennsylvania, Baltimore, Maryland, Washington D.C., and Richmond, Virginia before finally arriving in Georgia seventeen hours later. Both in York and Baltimore I stepped off of one bus, was pointed in a direction, and got on the next and kept going. It was pretty easy. In Washington D.C., though, I had a layover. I guess I hadn't really thought about the fact that I might not be able to just keep traveling continuously, and I really didn't want to go into the station.

I asked the driver what time my bus for Richmond would be leaving and he said, "How would I know? That's why they have the screens inside!"

I just wanted some help, so I said, "Well, how do I use the screens? I don't even know what I'm looking for!"

He said, "You'll figure it out, country boy," and he walked away, leaving me outside the station staring at the mass of people rushing around to catch their buses.

Confused, I walked around the bustle of the enormous station. I found the screens that the driver told me about. They had listed cities, and had columns indicating "arrivals," "departures," and "Gate numbers." As I stared at the screen pretending to know what I was doing, a skinny, young, white guy in his twenties came over and stood next to me. Somehow he knew I was having trouble. Maybe it was the tears streaking down my face.

"Need some help, Chief?"

As I turned to my left, I found that he was talking to me. I resisted the urge to explain how much I hate being called "chief."

"Uh, yeah. I'm headed to Richmond next."

He carefully perused the screen, squinting along the way. "Let's see. . .Richmond. . .Richmond. . .There it is! Whoa! Looks like you have a good two hours to kill, Chief. Let's go get something to eat."

There was a Burger King located in the station, and I began to follow this skinny little guy because I didn't know what else to do. He was dressed in a full suit, but it looked liked he had kept it in his gym bag for the last few days. It had all kinds of creases in it and I wasn't sure that he hadn't purchased it out of a vending machine somewhere in the lobby. He had greasy hair pulled into a ponytail and a barely visible mustache; the kind people who can't grow facial hair wear in an attempt to look older. I remember letting my mustache grow for my first driver's license picture when

I was sixteen. I thought if I looked older in the photograph, that I might be served at some bars. The hair only grew at each end of my upper lip, and instead of passing for someone of legal drinking age, it looked like I had just finished a glass of kool-aid on the day the picture was taken.

I continued to follow "Slick" (that was my name for him) to the Burger King because I was hungry. But I was also on my guard. I wasn't ready to trust anyone on this trip, especially not this guy. But as I watched him, I decided that I could take him if I had to. Isn't it funny how men always judge each other based on whether or not we can "take" each other?

Secure again in my masculinity, I ordered a Whopper. As I slurped my shake, I listened to Slick's stories.

"Yeah. My grandfather is a billionaire. He's just loaded! He's got six limousines and everything. Yeah, he's going to fund the bar I'm opening down in Kentucky. Oh, I forgot to tell you, I have a degree from Kentucky. I own a house down there. Anyway, I have this degree in business management, so I appointed myself the manager of this bar. It'll do great. I have an excellent business sense."

I figured if he was talking about being good at shoveling BS, he was right.

"I just bought this new car for my girlfriend. Paid cash. She really deserves it, though. She's a recovering drug addict, but I'm going to give her everything. You know what I mean?. . .You pack heat?"

I hadn't really been paying close attention to his stories. It was obvious that he was making them up, and that he was trying to impress me. Even though I didn't believe a word he was saying, I perked up at his last sentence.

"What? What are you talking about?" I figured he was talking about a gun, but I wanted to be sure.

"Heat. You know, a gun. Do you carry a gun?"

"No."

"Well, be careful out there, man. I used to carry a gun everywhere. A .45, man. Now I just have my knife. I really don't need it, though. I'm a black belt in karate."

Well, that was enough. I just wanted to get away from this moron. I felt like telling him the only reason I would need a gun would to be to blow my brains out listening to his inane stories.

"I'm going to get in line," I said, politely but firmly. I felt I had been a good sport in all this, but every man has a breaking point. I wanted to leave this guy behind and move forward with my travels.

I hoped we had parted ways for good, but he followed me to my departure exit and stood in line with me. He started playing love songs that his girlfriend had recorded for him on a hand held tape player. I was going crazy. Finally, my bus arrived. I felt relief, like a man who had received a jug of water after days in the desert.

Slick walked me to the door and shook my hand. I felt a little guilty at my anger towards him. He was probably just a lonely, insecure traveler that needed someone to listen to his stories. I probably shouldn't have been so hard on him. Guys like him make me nervous, though. The type that just keep shooting their mouths off, because that is all they've ever known. That's fine if they are on their own. But when they are with me, they might pop off to someone and expect me to back them up.

"Take it easy, Chief," I said, as we parted ways.

As I walked through the gate, I handed the bus driver my ticket. He examined it, approved it, and pointed me in the direction of my bus. As I stood there stuffing my ticket into my back pocket, the guy behind me in line handed his ticket to the driver. The driver refused to accept it, "Sorry, the bus is full.

Incredulously, the guy behind me said, "What do you mean?"

The driver, who was finishing up his cigarette, nonchalantly said, "It's full. There aren't any more seats. You'll have to wait for the next bus to Virginia."

The guy said, "Well, when is it?"

As he stamped out his cigarette butt, he stated, "Six or seven hours from now."

The entire row of people behind me erupted in anger.

"What the #!@*& do you mean 'six or seven' hours? What the #!@*& are we supposed to do until then?"

The driver smiled as he pulled the door to the departure exit behind him, "Have fun!"

I was amazed at this stroke of luck so early in my trip. I was one person away from being stuck in this station for another seven hours! I felt like I had made a mistake taking this trip since getting out of my parents' car, but now I started thinking that maybe this was my destiny. Perhaps this was exactly what I was supposed to be doing, and perhaps I would meet a person who would connect me to an awesome, exciting career. Maybe I'll meet someone famous who will hook me up with a sweet offer to be a personal assistant. Even better, maybe I'll meet some hot chick, we'll fall in love and spend the rest of our lives together!

The possibilities seemed endless. There was a change in my countenance as I approached the bus. Maybe I hadn't made a mistake in taking this trip.

Because I had spent so much time at Slick's Burger King Story Hour, I was the last one getting to board the bus. I waited patiently as the riders in front of me searched for their seats and crammed their belongings in the overhead compartments. I was getting excited about who my riding partner might be. Being the last one on the bus confirmed for me that destiny would decide who I would sit with.

I was giddy with excitement when I finally put my foot on the first step. The line was still moving slowly as people continued to search for seats. I took another step. One more step to go.

Finally, I was standing in the front of the bus, looking back at all the faces and all the seats. "Where's mine?" I wondered. I just stood there, because I really couldn't do anything until the people ahead of me found their seats. My anticipation was high, as I waited for that last empty seat that would proclaim, "Quay, once you sit in this seat, nothing will ever be the same again!" Of all the things my destiny could be, I was really hoping it would involve a hot chick.

People gradually took their seats, and soon I was the last person standing. I walked more than halfway back the aisle looking for my seat. It was obvious, though, that every spot was taken. I turned around, banging my huge duffel bag against the heads of the people on either side of me as I moved.

I slowly started moving back towards the front of the bus in search of my seat. I looked left and right, searching for the open seat meant for me, but I couldn't find it. The riders were getting restless, because the driver would not pull out until I was seated. The driver had also turned off the lights in anticipation of our departure, which made it all the more difficult to find my spot. I was embarrassed as I struggled to get down the aisle with my bag, looking for my seat. I turned around at one point to be sure the bus really was full.

I began to get upset. Maybe the driver had miscounted and there was no room for me on this bus. If that were true, then all my dreams about this being my "destiny" seemed silly, since I wasn't even really supposed to be on this bus. All of the excitement and hope I had moments ago faded as I once again thought that maybe this was all a big mistake.

"Just sit down!" someone yelled.

"You're holding everything up!" another chimed in.

"Haven't you ever been on a bus before?"

I returned to the boarding point at the front of the bus. The driver must have been wrong. I accepted the fact that I was not supposed to be on this bus after all. As I prepared to get off, I heard a voice call out from row four, "I have a seat right here, young fella'." I looked back, and there sat on old, black guy.

"Right here is a seat for you, Buddy," he repeated, as he moved over towards the window. Apparently, he had been sitting in the aisle seat, and I didn't see that the seat by the window was vacant.

I reluctantly went to row four, stuffed my belongings under the seat and sat there facing forward.

What about my destiny? I was supposed to be sitting with someone who was going to advance my career, offer me something no one else could, or meet the woman of my dreams. There were a lot of options in my plans, but this certainly was not one of them.

As the driver backed away from the building, he ran through his perfunctory announcements: "radios are forbidden unless you have headphones, watch your language, and the scheduled time of arrival in Richmond is four hours from now." At the end of these announcements, he stated, "Now, say hello to the new friend sitting beside you."

I wouldn't look over. I wanted nothing to do with the man beside me. I figured some old, black guy did not want anything to do with me either. We would sit here for the next four hours and part ways in Richmond.

As much as I tried to avoid it, though, the black guy was looking at me. I think he knew that I was trying to ignore him or maybe he just thought I was shy. Either way, he said, "How ya' doin'?"

I looked sheepishly to my right. There he sat, smiling.

I thought, What does he want from me? It's obvious that we have nothing in common. He has to be in his late sixties, early seventies, he isn't from Pennsylvania, and he's black! What on earth could we possibly talk about? Despite my views on race, I was raised to be polite, so though I didn't have much to say, I replied, "I'm fine. How are you?"

"I'm good. Thanks for sitting with me. It's a long trip with no one to talk to. Things go a lot faster with a riding partner."

Oh, great. Now he wanted to be pals.

He continued, "Where ya' from and where ya' going?"

"Uh, I'm from Lancaster, Pennsylvania and I'm going to Atlanta."

"Lancaster! Amish country! It's beautiful up there! I'm from down here in D.C., but me and my wife used to go up there a lot before she died."

I hate when a stranger tells you someone close to them has died. Are you supposed to say you're sorry, even though you don't know them or the dead person? Besides, why would he offer this bit of personal information so early in our conversation?

"Yeah, Lancaster's nice. I'm actually from Strasburg, though. The city isn't really my thing."

Now I was the one offering personal information. Why was I doing that?

"The city's not for everyone, young man. The country isn't for everyone either. We tend to grow acclimated to whatever environment surrounds us. It's natural to be uncomfortable in places we've never been before. That's why I'm glad you had a chance to sit with me. You may not be used to all us city folk, but at least you now have one friend from Washington, D.C."

He already considered us friends. I thought that was strange. He didn't know anything about me, and now we were friends? If he knew how I felt about black people, he wouldn't want to be my friend.

"How did you know that I was uncomfortable when I got on this bus?" I asked him.

"It was in your eyes, Son. You can learn a lot about people as you look into their eyes. Their strengths. Their fears. Their ambitions. Some say that the eyes are the windows to the soul. Besides, you don't look like you're from around here. The bus can be a scary place for a first time traveler. I'm glad I had a seat open for you."

"I wasn't scared," I stated, fearfully.

We continued to talk. It was a four hour ride to Richmond,

so we had plenty of time. We discussed everything, and although I can't say that I became completely comfortable at any point, I was definitely more relaxed than I ever thought I would be in this situation.

We must have looked awfully strange on that bus. This guy was almost seventy, and I was twenty-three. He was from Washington, D.C. and I was from Strasburg, Pennsylvania. He was black and I was white. But there we sat, just talking.

My riding partner began explaining what it was like in Washington D.C. when he was my age, and schools were desegregating. Those of us who didn't live during the civil rights movement tend to forget that it happened relatively recently.

"You know, Son, I wouldn't have even been able to sit up here when I was your age. That's why I always sit near the front. It wasn't all that long ago when I couldn't.

It was tough during the fifties. Lot of hatred going around, and D.C. was always at the center of things, since that's where the government functions. I remember in 1952 how the Klan came to town to protest the possibility of desegregation in the schools. There were thousands of them marching down the street in their robes and hoods. It was scary, but also very exhilarating. I just wanted freedom, ya' know? This was supposedly a free country, and I couldn't get a drink in the same water fountain as other folks. That just didn't seem right.

Man, it was tough at that time! You always had to watch your back."

I was familiar with the march he was talking about. We had watched a video about it in one of my college classes. I never completely understood the movement. If I was black, I think I would have just asked for a separate nation. It was obvious that blacks and whites were never going to get along in this country, so why not make separate but equal, truly "separate and equal?" In fact, as I watched that march, I could sympathize with the Klan. These guys were watching their country fall to pieces. The Klan was comprised of a lot of poor, white men who never got a break in their lives. Yet, here were blacks demanding "equal rights," when it was painfully obvious that even poor whites didn't really have equal rights. I understood what the Klan was saying.

As I sat on the bus listening to my riding partner, though, I could also see what he was saying. It's true that it seemed awfully hypocritical for the primary political document of a country to say, "All men are created equal," while it blatantly denied equality to a segment of its citizens. In fact, as my partner talked, I visualized the leader of the Klan at that march screaming into his microphone. Oddly enough, the members of the Klan were probably more like the blacks they hated than they thought. Maybe that was their primary motivation, jealousy; Blacks were going to have what even poor whites didn't yet possess.

As I thought about that klansman screaming into his microphone, I had a thought. What if he and my riding partner had crossed paths that day in D.C.? Would the klansman have thought differently? My riding partner was nothing like the stereotypes that the Klan used for blacks. Is there a possibility he would have thought differently? Would he have even given him a chance?

I felt bad as we rolled into Richmond. My riding partner had been talking for the last hour about his experiences at my age, yet I had been daydreaming about the possibilities of that fictional meeting between him and the klansman. It probably wouldn't have changed him, I figured. You have to be willing to challenge your views before you are open to listening to others.

As my riding partner and I arrived at the station, we went our separate ways to find separate buses to our separate destinations. Unfortunately, after getting off the bus I never saw him again. Never even got his name. Even though I had been thinking about other things during the end of trip, I wanted to thank him for making me feel comfortable. I didn't expect it, especially from a black guy. He didn't have to do that for me, but he did, and I appreciated it.

I transferred onto my last bus before Atlanta. It was night, and all I wanted to do was sleep. And that I did. We arrived in Atlanta that next morning. I had survived the first leg of the journey. Time to hit the city.

2

As my days passed in Atlanta, I started to think about my next destination and the ride to get there. And then the next one. And then the next one. Though, I hadn't been traveling long, I could already see the attraction to life on the road. I didn't want to look past where I was, but the freedom to come and go as I pleased was an intoxicating feeling, and one that I still savor. I was relaying these impressions to my friend as he drove me to the bus station. I thought he would be happy for me, but instead he had a grim look on his face.

"What's wrong with you?" I inquired.

"Just be careful. All right?"

"What are you talking about?" I asked defensively.

"You, and this whole . . . adventure, or whatever the #!@*& you call it! Nothing personal, but you don't know what the #!@*& you're doing. You're just a hillbilly and traveling around to all these cities is not safe for a guy like you."

I knew there was some truth to what he was saying, but I found it insulting for him to think that I couldn't handle it.

"Hey, I'm a big boy, OK? I can take care of myself."

"No, you can't! Look, Quay, I'm from Philly. I know who the bad guys are. I know who to trust and who not to trust. I've been in hundreds of fights, so I know how to defend myself. You don't know what you're getting yourself into."

"Fine. Then I would rather die trying than to sit at home and never experience life!"

"That's exactly what's going to happen if you're not careful."

"I'll be fine! Just leave me the #!@*& alone!"

My friend was quiet the rest of the way. As he pulled into the fire lane in front of the Atlanta Greyhound, he offered me one last bit of advice.

"Listen, you do whatever the #!@*& you want, OK? Just do me one favor. If you get lost, don't know what to do, are having trouble with something, whatever, just don't ask any blacks for help, OK? These city blacks are not like the people you know. They're like animals. They'll tear up a stupid hick like you."

"Fine," I said, exasperated. "I wouldn't ask them for help anyway."

We shook hands and parted ways.

The Atlanta station was bustling with activity. Using my newly acquired skill for reading the departure screens, I quickly determined the gate number for my departure. I had over an hour to wait, so I wrote in my journal as I sat in line. My experience in Washington D.C. taught me that in order to guarantee myself a seat, I needed to be in line as early as possible.

I wrote for a while, but then just packed my belongings and contemplated my next destination. I was going to Florida to spend the week with my grandparents. They weren't my grandparents by blood, but they had raised my father. Having grown up with these people next door, I had some reservations about our visit. I wasn't worried about Nan. She was one of the sweetest most gentle persons that I knew. It was grandpa that gave me reason to pause. He could be too old-school for my taste.

By 6:00 p.m. I was boarding a bus bound for the Sunshine State.

I picked a seat near the back and began to notice that most of the riders were in "defensive passenger mode." This was a name I gave to the practice of solo riders attempting to deter boarding passengers from sitting with them. The goal of a solo passenger is to have two seats to himself, therefore making sleep easier. In "defensive passenger mode" (from here on referred to as *dpm*) the passenger piles stuff on the seat next to him and continually looks back at the bathroom, as if waiting for someone to return. It often worked. Another method passengers in *dpm* employed was to feign sleep or talk aloud in order to appear crazy. "Stuff piling," however, was the most popular method.

The rider in front of me was around twenty-eight and dressed like he was on the PBR rodeo circuit. He had on worn gray boots, but I wouldn't have imagined him as a bronco buster. His shirt was one of those western kind where the top is a different color than the bottom. It connected up the front with simulated marble snaps instead of buttons. He had a nice looking cowboy hat on, and I guessed him to be from Texas, but he talked with an accent that I would later discover to be from northern Florida.

The Florida Kid was in full *dpm*, and told me that this trip would be "sweet" if he managed to secure his own seat the whole way to Jacksonville. Just about the moment he got those words out, we both looked forward to see a nice looking girl boarding the bus. When she stepped on the bus, her figure immediately stood out as something to behold. She was athletically built, almost muscular, which is still more appealing than thin if you ask me, and her long blond hair was scraggly from the rain, in a cute sort of way.

Attractive women on the bus were few and far between. I had already realized this, even though I had not been riding the bus very long. Her appearance was quite an event. When my new friend saw her board, his eyes lit up. She was encountering lots of people in *dpm*, so by the time she got to our section, she was ripe for the picking. The Florida Kid quickly moved his stuff, and when Venus was next to him he offered her a seat. She obliged. I was a bit distraught, as I shuffled my pile, but upon closer inspection, I was glad the Kid got his lasso around her before I did.

The two began talking immediately, and since I had met the Kid earlier, he did me the pleasure of including me in the conversation.

"Emma, this here is Clay. He's from Pennsylvania."

"Pennsylvania? Ever see any vampires, Clay?"

I know my name is difficult, but I absolutely hate it when people call me Clay. And the joke (or was she serious?) about vampires. Come on. Give me a break.

"Uh, the name is Quay. With a Q. And I believe you're thinking of Transylvania when you reference vampires."

"Oh yeah," she replied with a dreamy voice as she looked lovingly into the eyes of the Kid.

It wasn't long before I began to feel like a third wheel, or in this case, a saddlesore, so I just sat back and faded out of the conversation. They didn't notice at all.

I listened to their foreplay conversation. It centered on alcohol and food, which led them into some kind of philosophy on love and sex, or something like that. I was trying not to pay too much attention. Anyway, as dusk began to shroud the bus, the two moved closer together. I imagined them pretending they were on the bench seat of his pick-up truck, his left hand on the wheel, his right arm around her. The image was complete when I pictured a gun-rack spanning the width of their heads, and a sticker of Calvin pissing on a Ford symbol.

It wasn't long before they started doing things one would have trouble doing while in the front seat of his heavy Chevy.

We arrived in Jacksonville around 2:30 in the morning.

My first observation was the parting of the Kid and Venus. I imagined a scene right out of a movie where they wander off the bus, hand in hand, the wind blowing her now greasy hair, as they run in slow motion towards the ocean. Well, he ran all right - straight to his departure exit. Maybe they said their good-byes on the bus. Maybe he had told her he loved her and their paths would cross again. But when he got to that Jacksonville bus station there was only one thing on his mind; his next bus.

I saw Venus standing with another woman, somebody who hadn't been on our bus. They were exchanging salutations, and I assumed she was picking up Venus. The Kid rushed by without saying a word. To be honest, I don't even think they saw each other. Their relationship ended without so much as good-bye, as did most friendships started on the bus. As I witnessed this, I thought it to be strange and sad. But then I realized it was probably an accurate reflection of most human relationships.

My memory took me back to the friends I had made in college and high school, even elementary school. How few with whom I still had contact! I remembered the last time I had seen them, and how grandiose I would have made the good-bye if I'd known that would be the end.

But the friends and the encounters we have in life often serve the purpose of getting us from one phase to the next, just as the friend I met on the bus got me from Pennsylvania to Atlanta. Some friends are lasting, some temporary, but all are important. Although it saddened me to think of all the people in my life who I no longer communicated with, I found solace in knowing that somehow we served each other's purpose. In ten years these people from the bus will be memories as well, but that did not take away from the present importance they were having in my life.

Content with these thoughts, I sat down in one of a string of connected seats. Each seat had its own TV, which I thought to be cutting edge technology. I was intent on finding some good programming to entertain myself during the layover. When I found it was going to cost me a quarter for every five minutes, I realized that watching a full movie would be more expensive than going to the theater. So much for cutting edge.

I got even more disgusted when I realized that the television only had one channel. I hit it several times to see if it would pick up any other stations, but this only loosened the two screws holding it in place.

As I watched an infomercial with Fran Tarkenton on the now wobbly screen, I felt someone peering over my shoulder. I turned to my left, and there sat an old, black guy, watching my TV.

"How ya' doin'?" he said.

"Okay," I replied.

I figured he was homeless and was hanging out here in the

bus station. I tried to focus on the screen, but he kept laughing and making comments about what was going on. "You probably don't remember him, young man, but that Fran Tarkenton was a heck of a football player. A heck of a player!"

I was feeling very uncomfortable. The station wasn't very big, and it seemed like a lot of people were looking at me, because the black guy was speaking very loudly. I had never actually talked to a homeless guy before. In fact, the only one I could ever remember even seeing was during a tour of New York I had taken with a group from Lancaster. The thing I remember about the NY Homeless Guy was that he puked all over the place when we walked by. I figured that's what homeless people do; they puke on the tourists.

The Jacksonville Homeless Guy wasn't puking on me yet, but he was really annoying me, so I pulled a quarter out of my pocket, and gave it to him. "There. Now you can watch your own TV." He stared at me with a look like, "You don't think you're going to get off that easily, do you?"

"Thank you. Thank you. But I'm not going to waste that on the TV. I'm going to put it right here," and he proceeded to place it in the breast pocket of his flannel shirt.

I could care less what he did with it at this point. My own television had run out of time, and I was ready to go over and stand in line. Then, before I could get up, he grabbed my arm and said, "Let me tell you my story."

He pulled out a Florida driver's license.

"You see this? That's all I have left. I fell asleep while I was waiting for my bus this afternoon and I had $300 stolen out of my pockets. All they left me was my license."

I didn't doubt that this could have been a possibility. But I didn't believe him. I guess mainly because I couldn't imagine the robbers taking the time to remove just his license from his wallet, all the while not waking him up.

"I had put my stuff in one of those lockers over there, but

they stole the key to that, too. I need to get into that locker to get my brother's phone number so he can come and get me."

Many Greyhound stations have small lockers that a rider can deposit a quarter in, lock, and pull the key out. You can keep your stuff in there for up to twenty-four hours, but if you lose the key, it costs ten dollars to get the station manager to open it back up. At this time of night, though, there was no one who could open the lockers.

I started to realize that I was dealing with a crafty fellow. He wanted ten dollars so he could get someone to open the locker come daybreak. By then, though, I'd be long gone so there would be no way I could be sure that's what he was using it for. I gave him the fifty cents I had in my pocket.

"That's all I have."

"Thank you. Thank you. Are you sure you don't have any more?"

"I'm positive."

We sat in silence for a moment.

He mumbled, "I sure could use something to eat from that Burger King over there."

I got up and walked away. Enough was enough. All he wanted was money, and he wasn't getting any more of mine. After I left, I heard him say to the black guy behind me, "Say, bro' you got some change?"

I wondered why he didn't give that guy the story I heard. He just asked him for some money which was all he was looking for anyway. In time I came to realize that the homeless saved their "A" material for prime targets. I looked like a dumb country boy in the middle of the big city. I was young and inexperienced, so he thought I would probably fall for the old "had my wallet and key stolen" story. Well, he got fifty cents from me, but that was it. I guess I could consider that a win.

I was extremely tired by the time our bus arrived. It was

around 4:00 a.m. and I hadn't gotten a wink of sleep yet that night. As we boarded, I had high hopes of keeping my own seat, so I put my *dpm* into full effect. As I pretended not to see all the passengers walking by, I accidentally made eye contact with an unattractive younger lady sitting across the aisle from me. She had short, spikey, blond hair and wore a miniskirt made out of jean material, which was complemented by a thin, white halter top that made it painfully obvious that she wasn't wearing a bra. As we sat and talked about nothing important, someone wanted to sit with her. She promptly moved across the aisle and sat right on top of the stuff I was using for my *dpm*.

"Sorry I sat on your stuff," she said with a giggle. "Want to reach under and get it?"

Yikes.

"Uh, no. That's OK. You can just throw it under the seat for me."

I know you shouldn't judge a person based on her looks. We're all a prize catch for some, and for others we're fit for a doghouse. But it wasn't just her looks I found to be ugly. She constantly swore. I had only recently realized how ignorant it made one sound. My own language could be coarse, but coming from a woman it is not at all appealing, especially if she looks like Fido.

I sat there and listened to her swear for an hour or so, and finally pretended to fall asleep. I eventually did fall asleep, and when I awoke three hours later, my blond beauty was asleep too. I looked to my left to see the top of her spiked hair resting comfortably on my shoulder. I followed her arm down to find that her hand was on the inside of my thigh, about four inches from my crotch.

Not knowing what bus etiquette was concerning a riding partner molesting you while sleeping, I simply endured it for the remainder of the trip. She may have been dreaming about me, because she had this huge smile on her face and would occasionally adjust herself to get closer, which was virtually impossible unless she were to climb inside my shirt. When we arrived in Port St. Lucie, I eased myself out from under her hand and placed her bag under her head, just like Indiana Jones did with that statue in Raiders of the Lost Ark. She never even felt me leave.

3

I spent ten days with my grandparents in Port St. Lucie, Florida. I love them immensely, buy nobody should be subjected to that much time, day in and day out, with relatives. Especially not with grandparents. With such an age difference and nothing to talk about, all we did was eat. Grandparents still have the old fashioned belief in three big meals per day. I don't necessarily dislike it, but it can get to be overwhelming. I started to feel like food was constantly being rammed down my throat.

"Here, Quay, eat more beef! A real man needs his red meat! Have some more bread! It's homemade! You haven't finished your three gallons of mashed potatoes. What's the matter with you? Are you on a diet? Are you hungry for a stick of butter?"

I know, I know. I shouldn't complain. Up to that point, I was eating out of Greyhound stations on a consistent basis which is like digging through a trash can.

At the end of the visit my grandmother drove me, my duffel bag, and my fat gut to the bus station. I waddled onto the bus and found a seat. I wasn't sure if all the food had gone to my butt or what, but the seat felt tighter than normal.

I was headed to the University of Alabama where my high school friend Jon was going to college. I had felt a little cramped at my grandparents, so it was refreshing to get on the hot, smelly bus. I wasn't interested in talking to anybody or making any trite conversation, so I sat back and watched Florida go by through the window.

One of the pleasures of traveling alone was the moments like these. If I had traveled with somebody, he may have wanted to talk. Maybe he would get upset if I didn't. Or maybe later I would want to wax philosophic or something, and he would want to sleep. It could get difficult. While riding the bus I had the opportunity to do whatever struck me at the time. If I wanted to be alone, I just stared out the window and kept to myself. If I wanted to talk, I almost never had trouble finding someone to do so. But talking and not talking was truly a surface thing.

On a deeper level, traveling alone meant that I didn't have to be who I had always been. I know that sounds strange, but sometimes I think we base our decisions and beliefs on what we've always been. Just like sitting with that black guy on the first leg of this journey. I never would have done that back home. I never would have talked to that guy. And if any of my friends had seen me talking to him, they would have said, "What were you talking about with THAT guy?!"

On the bus, I felt free. I felt like I was starting over. I didn't know exactly who I wanted to be, but it was refreshing to know that I was starting with a blank slate with everyone I met. I stayed in my shell the whole way to Jacksonville.

I wandered around the Jacksonville station a bit, but soon headed to my departure exit, even though we weren't to be leaving for another two hours. Not only did I find an early arrival at the departure gate to be essential to securing a seat on the next bus, but it also gave me an opportunity to see who else would be riding on my bus. I could interact and talk with people that would be making the journey with me. If I knew it was going to be a full bus, I could ask a certain person to sit with me, thus ensuring myself a good riding partner. If someone was annoying, I would try and avoid sitting with that individual. It was just a good testing ground for potential riding partners.

When I arrived at my exit in Jacksonville, I was the fourth person in line. I sat on the floor, and as other riders arrived, the departure gate resembled a random gathering more than a line. We all sat in silence and listened to the soothing strains of the music overhead.

This particular bus station was large and drab, with few

windows. Our exit was at the end of the station, down a long aisle, and isolated from the rest of the building. There weren't many people around for such a big station, and I think part of the reason for our quietness was a fear that it would sound like Lou Gehrig's farewell speech if we dared to make a sound.

As I was picking at my fingernails avoiding eye contact with everybody, someone finally broke the silence with the standard question, "Where ya' headed?"

I looked up to find that the inquiry was directed at me, though the reverberation could have led someone on the other side of the building to think it was for him.

This guy was in his mid-twenties. He had a long blond mullet which was spiked at the top (spiked hair was still somewhat in style at that time, but fading fast). The fu-manchu mustache he had going was thick, but he didn't look that tough. He was rotund and his outfit wasn't doing anything to hide that fact. He had on a pair of those hideous Jams shorts, and a huge medical shirt. One of those loose fitting, V-neck things that fat people wear to try to hide their big bellies.

As he and I talked, the rest of the group joined in to listen, and a circle began to form on the floor. One by one, each person told where he or she was from and where he or she was headed. It began to resemble group therapy, with each one of us listening intently as the others talked. I was waiting for someone to stand up and say, "Hi, my name is Bob, and I'm a bus rider." And we would all answer, "Hi, Bob!"

The character with the most interesting story was the hefty guy who had started the whole discussion. He told us he was a "lighting engineer." This quickly brought a smile to my face as I imagined him scaling the ceiling of Madison Square Garden. I pictured him with a string of lights in one hand, the other hand hanging on for dear life as the I-beam began to bend, and the people below getting showered with Hershey kisses falling out of the pockets of his Jams. I continued to laugh even though he told us he wasn't involved in the construction aspect of the job, but in designing the shows on his computer. He rattled off the names of Metallica, REO Speedwagon, and U2 as some of his clients.

I found this all very interesting, but my mind kept going back to Slick and his fantastic stories. This guy was just like him. He was sitting there handing us a bunch of crap about being some big wig engineer, and here he was riding the bus like the rest of us schlepps. I wasn't ready to buy into this guy yet.

He went on to tell some specific things about shows and I finally got the nerve to call his bluff.

"If you're doing so well with all these concerts, why in the world are you riding the bus? I would imagine Metallica could afford to send you on a plane."

I know it sounded harsh, but I wanted to reveal him as a sham.

The group seemed shocked at my question, but they were probably just as curious as I. We all sat silently staring at him, waiting for his answer. He looked at me and the rest of the group, and then looked down in embarrassment. His pudgy face turned red as he stammered to tell us why.

"I know it sounds stupid, but I'm deathly afraid of flying. I'll take the long road of travel any day to avoid getting on a plane. I have my equipment sent ahead by air. But me, I take the bus."

Everyone looked at me with anger in their eyes like I was some kind of insensitive jerk. Oftentimes, I was an insensitive jerk, and this time I knew it.

Now that everyone realized he was legitimate, they were interested in hearing his stories about hobnobbing with rich and famous musicians. I was feeling jealous as I thought about the life he was leading. Traveling. Hanging out with rock groups. Making money. I wanted a piece of that action. I thought that maybe this guy was put in my life to take me with him. To see the world, and get paid doing it. A life of adventure! Who could ask for more?

I decided to hit him up for a job. I was feeling really bad

about calling him out, because I was afraid he would hold it against me, but I was bold nonetheless.

"Do you need anybody for your crew? I know how to do a lot of things."

"Nope. I only do the computer part of the job, and then I become a foreman when I get there. Each place hires their own people."

Undaunted, I proceeded forward.

"Well, do you know anybody who's looking for someone? Any stadiums? Any technicians? I'm telling you, I know a lot of stuff."

I really knew nothing about computers, electricity, lights, music, sound, instruments, art, pyrotechnics, acoustics, bass, treble, woofers, tweeters, or megabytes. But he didn't need to know that.

"Nope. You'd have to talk to them."

"Well, don't you need somebody to ride the plane with your computer to make sure it gets to the right place and that nobody screws it up?"

I must have been getting desperate. I was now willing to be a computer's babysitter.

"Nope. Got somebody who takes care of that."

"Do you have anything for me? I could give you my resume."

I had made a really bad resume before I left Pennsylvania. It was awful. I hated the way resumes were written. People always tried to make their blue collar jobs sound really fancy. For example, "construction worker" becomes, "Self-supervised labor officer requiring knowledge of physics, mathematics, and the English language." Me, I hate unnecessary ostentation. Just tell it like it is. I was proud that I knew how to run a tractor, and if that wasn't good enough for a resume reader, I didn't want to work for him or her. That's how I feel. As if an employer can judge the character and work ethic of a man from a piece of paper full of embellishments.

Resumes. I hated what they stood for. But I must have bought into it somewhat, since I made one to take with me on my trip. My thinking was that if I met somebody important, I would have something official to give him so he would remember me. About the only thing my resume would have reminded him is how *not* to write a resume.

After plenty of badgering, Computer Whiz agreed to take one of my resumes, more than likely just in case he ever ran out of toilet paper during his travels.

The group discussion continued until the arrival of the bus. No one else ever joined us down in our section of the station, so it was only eight of us going to Tallahassee. The bus had arrived with about fifteen passengers, so it would only be half full. A Greyhound holds forty-seven people; eleven rows with a pair of seats on each side of the aisle and a lone back seat that can hold three.

Although the group had gotten along well at the station, once on board we all grew tired and faded off to sleep. When the bus wasn't crowded or full of kids it could be extremely peaceful. The gentle hum relaxed me and late at night it was wonderful to leave the driving to Greyhound. I stretched out in the two seats I had and enjoyed the solitude.

At this point of my trip, I had figured out how to get into a good sleeping position. It was interesting to watch how other riders tried to get in just the right spot. Some people would lie flat on their backs with their legs bent at the knees and hanging in the aisle. Others would lie on their sides in the fetal position. Some would sit on the inside and prop their head against the window, using a sweatshirt or something as a pillow. Some people would lay right on the floor.

If I had both of the seats to myself, I would lay on my back with my head towards the aisle. I would then fold my legs Indian style and put them against the window. In other words, I formed myself into an L, legs up. It sounds really uncomfortable when described, but I spent many a night in that position.

I drifted in and out of sleep. I enjoyed the calm of the road like it was a gentle, caressing body of water taking me to the places I had always dreamed. The only thing that would have made it any better was a for a beautiful woman to sit beside me, and nestle up close as we drove into the night.

When we rolled into Tallahassee, the streets were empty, there was a little drizzle and traffic was light. This made sense since it was after midnight on a Thursday. I was swimming in relaxation, happy to be at this point and time in my life.

The layover in Tallahassee was brutal. Several buses had broken down, so there was a huge backlog at the station. The place was packed with hot, sweaty Floridians. At one point I had gone into the bathroom, and there were these scummy looking guys drinking beer. I have enough trouble trying to pee in a urinal next to someone, let alone being on display in this makeshift bar. I did the best I could, and was soon to board my next bus.

My bus arrived in Tallahassee at 3:00 a.m., a good two hours behind schedule, and I boarded for the next leg of the journey to Birmingham, Alabama. I took a seat near the back, and because of the few riders I had no need to implement my *dpm*. I wasn't really tired since I had drank a good six or seven coffees at the station (they had offered us free beverages for the inconvenience), so I sat and looked out the window.

Across the aisle from me sat a small, thin man. He was not dressed like a typical bus rider. He had on nice pleated pants, an oxford shirt, and a sleeveless cotton vest. His shoes were those fancy kind with the little tassels hanging in the place of shoelaces. On the top of his head he wore a red beret, the first time I had ever seen a man wearing one other than in the movies. I had first noticed him in the station not only because of his funny headgear, but because he was carrying big, long tubes, the kind you use to transport posters.

There was more about this guy than just his non-typical bus clothing and tubes. He had this simple look of contentment on his face. There wasn't the appearance of frustration and anger that all the rest of us were wearing after the taxing wait in Tallahassee. He wasn't sweating either. I have always been a profuse sweater, so it didn't surprise me that the entire brim of my baseball cap was soaked clear through. That beret he had on was made of wool, but this guy didn't have a drop on him. If I would have been wearing that beret. . . .never mind. I'd never be wearing a beret.

He sat calmly, neither sleeping nor awake, in a kind of trance from the hum of the bus. Since I knew it would take a while for me to relax, I decided to get this guy's story. There had to be a reason behind his peace. I broke his trance with the standard, "Where are you headed?"

"Tennessee." His answer was short and not overly friendly, I think more because he was surprised then because he didn't want to talk.

"Is that your home?"

"Yes. Yes it is. Well, it's my home now. I'm actually from Peru. But I've lived here in the States for a pretty long time. The name is Pablo, by the way."

"Mine's Quay."

"Nice to meet you, Clay," he said as we shook hands.

"It's Quay, with a Q. Peru, huh? I've always wanted to see Peru." I was lying. At that point in my life I'm not exactly sure I could even locate Peru on a map, but I wanted to get his story, and I figured he'd feel more comfortable if I said something like that. More likely, he saw right through me, but he continued on anyway.

"My father moved our family here when I was about ten. I was a pretty good artist, and he felt that I would have a better chance of using it in America. Oh, did I love to draw! Father felt it would be best for me to become an architect, so he sent me to a good school and sure enough, I became an architect."

He presented it so simply and it sounded like everything

went just as planned. But his voice let on that there was much more to this story.

"You don't sound very happy about it, though."

I had found in my bus travels that people were extremely willing to open up to strangers. I would probably never say something like this in "regular" society without expecting him to reply, "It's really none of your business." On the bus though, people wanted to talk. People wanted to reveal their feelings. Sometimes the bus was the safest place to do it, since we would most likely never see each other again. Every rider was trying to get to something or get away from something.

"I didn't want to be an architect. I wanted to paint. I wanted to study art. I wanted to be a real artist, not some cog in an oversized company, where style is frowned upon and standard practice is rewarded. The more I did it, the more I realized; this isn't art. I'm completely under their control. I'm nobody."

"Well, why did you stay?"

He adjusted his beret a little as he looked vacantly ahead, seemingly ashamed.

"Once you start making that kind of money, it's easy to get spoiled. Every time I wanted to get out of it, something was thrown in my face as a reminder to why I needed it. Bills to pay. Repairs around the house. Trying to compete with the neighbors. To have the 'stuff,' I was selling my soul. My father was happy with my 'success,' but I was miserable."

"So what happened?"

"I talked it over with my wife. We both knew this would be a huge decision. Actually, it took a couple months. My feelings did not go away. In fact, they grew stronger. Finally, I quit. What a glorious day that was! We knew that we could survive for a while on my wife's income, and hopefully my art would begin to sell. See, my wife and I are people of faith, but my father is not, so he didn't understand that I had to be true to my calling."

To be honest, I didn't exactly understand either. "What do

you mean, 'people of faith?'" I questioned.

"We are Christians. As Christians, we believe that God has given us certain gifts and we are called to use them for his glory. When we simply take the safe route, we are not heeding his call. I was called to use my talent to further His kingdom, instead, though I was using my knowledge and skills to simply make money. I think that is why I was so miserable."

I grew up in a Christian home, but had abandoned my religion and God about four years before this trip. Despite my upbringing, I had grown hostile towards Christianity. I just couldn't understand why someone like Jesus Christ would come to die on a cross for my sins. It didn't seem logical. And to put all this trust in something you cannot see seemed risky to me.

"So, what happened when you made this change?" I asked.

"The first thing that happened was that my perspective on what I 'needed" changed immensely. Break life down to its bare essentials and you can do a lot more. People think the status they gain from having 'things' sets them free, when in actuality, it's what bolts them down. It strips them of their freedom. You become a slave to one of two things; the money to get the things; or the work to make the money to get the things. It's easy to do, though. I know. I was there. Once you understand the purpose God has planned for you, you break free. The peace that comes is like no other! What satisfaction! To know you're a slave to no one other than to the One who knows all and sees all. "

Pablo was beaming. His uninhibited emotion worked in a strange combination with his unbelievable peace, and it made me think. He was like so many Christians that I had met, including my parents. There was an understanding about how life worked, and a satisfaction that trusting God would yield the proper life. I just hadn't made that connection in my own pursuit of Christianity. To me, it just seemed like a lot of rules I had to follow, and once I realized I couldn't follow them, I just abandoned the whole thing. Pablo was giving me a different perspective, though.

"Are you a believer?" he asked.

"Well, I know a lot of stuff about God and Jesus and all that. I grew up in a Christian home. But I don't really buy into it anymore. I just have a lot of questions."

Pablo smiled.

"Just don't stop asking questions. The truth will be revealed if you continue to seek."

Some of the things he was saying did make sense, though. He was talking about a lot of the same things I had kicked around before I left on this trip. Sometime in your life, you had to make a decision before it was too late to turn back. For me, it was right when I left on this trip. I realized I was sacrificing the beginning of my "career" by not taking a "real job." Despite my pride in "living for the moment," I was thinking ahead to what would be best for me. I knew that taking a career job would be so appealing at first. Paid health insurance. Salary. Scheduled working hours. More money as time went on. Basically, everything a man needs to take the steps toward a "normal" life.

Right now though, I wanted to see the country. I had absolutely nothing to lose, despite what people claimed I did. Never again would I be able to do this without really sacrificing a lot. I couldn't take time off from my job to see the country, especially if I had house payments, or a wife, or a bunch of stuff I was still paying for. Right now, I could go broke and it wouldn't matter. I didn't want to wear a tie. I didn't want to work nine to five. I didn't want to settle down. I had forever to do that.

I just wanted to be absolutely sure before I took that step where I couldn't turn back. Maybe today I'm thinking, "I want to get started on my career." When I am forty, it might be different. By then it's too late. I knew that I would always have this adventure, even if I were to wake up tomorrow and find myself in a tie and punching the clock. This trip could never be taken from me.

After Pablo and I had re-sparked and encouraged each other,

we both faded off to sleep. I found it refreshing to meet someone a little bit older who could see where I was coming from. Perhaps he was happy to find someone a little bit younger out there who was searching as well.

4

After an extended weekend with Jon in Tuscaloosa, I prepared for my next stop. I had decided on Dallas, and had two good reasons to choose it for my next destination. For one thing, my Uncle Dick and his family lived there. For another, the Dallas Cowboys, who had won the Super Bowl that year, were having a celebratory parade. I knew, if I worked the schedule correctly, I could roll into Dallas just in time for the parade. Don't get me wrong. I'm a diehard Eagles fan, but figuring it would be a long time before they would be having any parades, I thought attending this would be exciting.

I left Tuscaloosa at 5:00 that afternoon, and I was due in Dallas the next morning around 7:00 a.m..

The journey to Dallas was going to be an interesting one. One of the very first stops on the way was in Mississippi. I knew there were a lot of black people living in the South, and although I had had mostly positive experiences with people of color thus far in the trip, I was concerned about being in Mississippi. I mean, there was a lot of racism in the state in the past. Would they accept some briar hopper like me? Would it be safe at the bus stations? Plus, I was worried about the Southern folk. I had always heard that they don't really like "Yankees." I was apprehensive about traveling there.

I boarded the bus and sat alone, pretty much sleeping the whole way to our first stop in Meridian, Mississippi. It was dark when we pulled into the station. The building was a one room square and it was so small that seven of us walking in and sitting down seemed to put it at half capacity. Most of the seats were right in the middle, lined up in traditional rows. On the left were several seats facing towards the rows, and there was another row in the very back, along the wall. I sat in the second row of the seats in the middle and decided to try and read.

Sure enough, I was just about the only white guy in the room. There was a black family of three sitting in front of me. It was an older family as the daughter was probably twenty-five years old. They were clad in Cowboys garb from head to toe, and I overheard them talking about the parade.

There was a black guy standing near the soda machine doing nothing. I was keeping my eye on him, but he seemed more bored than shifty to me. He kept digging in his pockets, I assume to try and find some change for a Coke. Two other fellows were roaming around the building, shuffling their feet. (It was only one room. They weren't too many places to shuffle.).

I must admit that Meridian gave me the creeps when we first got there. The weather was damp and foggy, and when I went to get some money from the ATM I found if very difficult to see. As I walked I began to sweat. It was uncomfortably warm, and as I peeled the layers off of me, I began to notice that I was the only white person around. I have to be honest, the whole scene made me uncomfortable.

In the station, everybody seemed to be minding their business. I was digging into a book since I hadn't done nearly as much reading as I had hoped to do thus far on the trip.

As I sat and read at the station, behind me I could hear a man telling stories. It bothered me, somewhat, that I had not seen him when I was measuring up the people within the station. This guy must have come in the back door or something, because I knew he wasn't on our bus from Tuscaloosa and the station was empty when we arrived. Maybe he was going to the bathroom when we got there. I wasn't sure. The station was deathly quiet, except for his low, coarse voice climbing over the silence. The words to his story faded in and out, in and out, but soon he came to the climax or something and though not loud, it was easily understood.

"I was tired of taking their #!@*&, so I pulled my gun. But they got a hold of me and threw me through the big window of the

#!@*& KMart. . .".

What?! What was this guy talking about? And who was he talking to? If he had a friend back there, it discouraged me even more because that meant I had missed two people in this tiny little station. One thing I had learned was to know and concentrate on my surroundings. Any station I went into, any bar, any store, I made a mental note of who was there and whom I may have wanted to keep an eye on. I was mad at myself for being irresponsible in letting these guys slip by undetected.

And what he was saying! I couldn't believe how he was spilling his guts right there in that station. All of us could hear it, and I saw a look of worry on the daughter's face in front of me. I'm sure she saw one on mine as well.

None of us dared to turn around though.

He continued on with his story.

"So the #!@*& police show up, and you know what they think of a black man with a gun. And I'm #!@*& cut all over and bleedin' from the window. And I'm yellin' at them, 'drop the #!@*& guns, you Pigs!' And they hollerin' back and I'm bleedin' all over the place." And on and on he went.

By now panic had spread through me. I wasn't sure what to make of this. It was obviously a story from the past. I figured that if it had happened that night, there would be blood on the floor or he wouldn't be sitting so calmly in the back of a bus station telling the story. And why was he telling this story now? Was he drunk? Was he crazy? My curiosity was starting to get the best of me.

I finally decided that I had to get a look at this guy. I felt it was important for me to know his physical characteristics, and to have an idea of exactly how close he was sitting to me. I also didn't want to accidentally sit next to him when we boarded the bus.

But what if I offended him? It might look like I wasn't minding my own business, which, well, I wasn't. What if he got really pissed and threw *me* through a window? What if he thinks I'm a cop? Then what? And I'm white. He didn't seem to like white people. It appeared that he wasn't thinking too rationally and I may have been asking for trouble, but my curiosity made me braver than I really was.

I turned slowly and cautiously, straining my eyes to the left until he came into my sight line. There he sat, totally alone, rattling off these stories to himself! I quickly returned to a face front position and opted to keep minding my own business. It wasn't long after that though, that he wanted to join the rest of us. He chose the seat one over from mine.

This guy, I'll call him passenger X, was a black man about five-foot-four, thin, and probably in his sixties. He walked very slowly, with a limp, and I couldn't tell if he had muscular dystrophy or was just drunk. He had on baggy blue pants, black shoes, and a sport coat that looked stained from years of soup spills. His head was like a raisin, wrinkled and indented in spots, the color broken up only by the graying scruff of his beard. The Brad Pitt look alike sported a derby upon his raisin, the brim sculpted in waves, and I shuddered to think of the tenants that resided there. He carried with him an old MacGregor gym bag, the zipper broken, exposing the junk he had collected.

Although his stature wasn't very intimidating, the fact that he had talked about having a gun (along with his being out of his mind), led me to believe that I should take necessary precautions.

I bought a cup of coffee. I know that sounds odd, but that was my weapon. That was my defense.

A lot of my friends couldn't believe that I would take a trip like this without some sort of weapon. Besides my rapier wit, that is. I'm not against guns or knives, just some of the idiots who have them. Anyway, I've never felt I needed one. They're more trouble than they are worth. But I did need my coffee. My feeling was, if trouble ever came about in a station, I would have a cup of hot coffee ready to throw into the person's face. Luckily I never had to do this, and I think I only ever bought coffee for that reason twice on this trip. This was one of them.

Passenger X kept to himself at first. The headphones to an old walkman hung around his neck, and I could hear that he had some country music on. He had his MacGregor bag sitting in the seat between him and me, and as best I could, I examined what it contained. I saw an old sweater, charcoal gray, that was once probably white. There was a squeeze bottle filled with I don't know what. It looked like a urine sample. There were rags and cans and paper in such a conglomeration, I had trouble distinguishing the end of one thing and the beginning of the next. It was basically a portable trash can.

I felt sympathy for X, though. He was obviously a very poor person, and his countenance made people fear him. Of course, it didn't help that he was talking about shooting cops either. We all just sat there, wary of X, but trying not to give him any undue attention. Soon a bus arrived from Atlanta, and three men came in and sat down. The one was a young, black man who sat in the line of seats along the wall, directly to the left of X and me. An older, neatly dressed, white guy went straight to the back, and sat in the row of seats back there. And the third guy, another young, black guy chose not to sit at all, but to stand away from the group, near the front door.

It was deathly silent. I couldn't believe there wasn't some music or something. It was the first time in my life I had wanted to hear the delightful strains of "Hey Jude" on the electric dulcimer. There was a feeling that something was going to happen by those of us who had been there, but the new guys were completely oblivious.

Suddenly, X turned to the young guy sitting in the seats to our left. After a short staredown, X blurted out;

"What?!"

Young Guy looked around as if there was someone else X could be addressing, but unmistakably, X was looking at him.

Young Guy just didn't respond.

X, pissed and disgusted, was not going to let Young Guy off

that easily. He stood up and walked towards him. Like I said, this place was small, so it was only about two steps or so.

"What, you mother#!@*&?!"

"I didn't say nothin'!" was Young Guy's strongest defense. Young Guy looked scared. He was much taller and broader than X, but we all were for that matter. There was sheer lunacy in X's voice, and I think we were all hoping he'd just pass out or something.

"Do you have somethin' to say, mother#!@*&? Huh?"

"I didn't say nothin'!"

Young Guy was more forceful this time, but his voice still lacked the confidence I thought it would take to get X off his back. X fumed for a moment, then he looked Young Guy square in the eye and said, "If I ever see you walking the streets of Jackson, Mississippi, I'll blow your #!@*& head off!"

My jaw dropped. The daughter in front of me let out a quiet shriek, and then whispered louder than she probably wanted to, "Dad, he's gonna' kill somebody!"

By this time, I had a pretty good caffeine high going, since I was on my third cup of coffee. My "cups of defense" kept getting cold, and I knew the only thing they would do to my predator was give him a good facial soaking. I was nervous, but unsure of what to do. Everybody stared, but no one said or did anything. X sat back down for the moment, and mumbled to himself. This was short lived, though. Soon he was back at it.

He rose to his knobby feet, housed by those dirty, black church shoes. I thought he was going to approach Young Guy again, but instead he drug his bad leg back to the older, white guy sitting in the back.

We all watched like witnesses to a car wreck.

"And what's your #!@*& problem, Whitey?!"

He got no reply. Older Guy just sat with his hands folded in his lap, looking past X as opposed to at him.

X raised his hand, as if to strike Older Guy. He pumped it

back and forth, and I waited to see that hand come down across the face and what was going to result from it. I must admit, Older Guy was pretty gutsy and just kept looking past X, as if he wasn't even there. I, personally, wanted someone to kick X's butt.

X offered Older Guy this warning;

"If I ever see you walking the streets of Jackson, Mississippi I'll blow your #!@*& head off!"

Like the last threat, no one said or did anything.

There wasn't any security in the building so no one was going to put a stop to this. Most bus stations only had security up until a certain time, usually 11:00 p.m.. I assumed this station was going to close after our bus arrived, because there was almost no one of authority there. Behind the counter stood one guy and he proceeded to nonchalantly tag bags, unaffected by the goings on.

One thing I noticed about Greyhound employees was that they seemed like the type of people who had seen it all. They were usually calm and collected. They didn't overreact to much of anything, especially drunks hanging around the station. More than likely X spent a lot of time there, and probably did the same type of thing on a nightly basis. It was business as usual to the Greyhound attendant. I was waiting for the employee to say to X, "Okay, Harold. That will be enough!"

The Greyhound employee might have been calm, but the rest of us were practically soiling ourselves. I deliberated for a bit and decided that if X touched me, I was going to lay him out. Don't get me wrong, I'm no particular tough guy, but I measured up my competition and figured I could take him. He was thin, old, and drunk. The only way he would beat me was with a gun. To me, though, he just seemed too feeble to be quick on the draw. I'd be ready.

X shuffled back to his seat for the time being, as we all sat in anticipation of what would happen next. There were no more violent outbursts, though X still made his rounds bothering everybody. For example, he offered the daughter the squeeze bottle

I had seen in his gym bag. She, of course, declined, but X wasn't quite done with his flirtation. He went back to his grab bag of goodies, and pulled out that sweater that must have doubled as an oil rag. This, too, he offered in a gesture of chivalry. This time the daughter said, "I don't want that crusty old thing either."

X responded, "I'm just going to throw it away then."

"Good," she replied.

X spent the rest of his time going around the station bothering people, but never saying anything threatening the rest of our time there. Actually, I think he said at least one thing to every single person in that place except for me. He must have noticed that I was armed with coffee.

The bus arrived for Jackson and everybody, including myself, breathed a sigh of relief. We could finally leave this guy behind and get on with the rest of our trip. I figured there was no way he could afford a candy bar, let alone a bus ticket. But sure enough, he lined up with us, flashed a ticket the same as us, and boarded with us.

I just couldn't believe it. Where in the world would he have gotten the money for a ride to Jackson? I met an older lady in Portland later in my trip who explained it to me. She had been riding the bus for thirty years. She said that certain undesirables hang out at every station. When they get to be too much, or that particular station is tired of them, the station gives the guy a one-way ticket to the next city. Then it becomes the next station's problem. A really crazy person would have an opportunity to see the whole country for free. Of course, he would also have to eat out of trash cans, so I'm not sure the trade-off would be worth it.

Our bus driver welcomed us onto his bus and talked about several scheduled stops. The daughter interrupted him to yell, "We ain't stoppin'! Just drive and get us there!"

All of us laughed as we felt the same way.

X didn't say any more until we were just outside the Jackson city limits. It was then that he woke the bus up by yelling; "There it is! There it is! Jackson, Mississippi!"

X got off the bus with his gym bag and began to hobble off into the night. I had a sad feeling as I watched him go. I wasn't one to feel sorry for people. I hated most people as a matter of fact. But, since the beginning of this trip, people just looked different to me. Why was I feeling this way? I guess I just wondered if there was more to X's story than his bus station rampages. I mean, where was he going? Did he have any family? What was his life like? I never thought like this before. It scared me to actually care.

The Jackson station was quite large compared to the one in Meridian. As I was getting my bearings, an announcement for a departure was made. A large, white man was making a ruckus as he headed for the departure exit.

"See y'all later! See ya! Bye!"

He waved his enormous hand and shouted until he reached the door. A moment later the people in the station started cheering and laughing with each other. I was a bit bewildered, and I asked a young, black guy who was sitting a seat down from me what had happened.

"That dude was crazy, man! He was in here buggin' everybody; shakin' peoples' hands; swearin'. He was weird, man! We're all glad just to see him go."

I laughed to myself as I thought of the strikingly similar situation we had just gone through in Meridian. Watching the celebration; the high-fives, the laughing and relaying of stories, it made me think of the special bond that formed between riders. Often, I encountered strange people in bus travel. I also witnessed a couple of moments that could have gotten out of hand. I certainly felt danger in these situations, but there was comfort in not being alone. Indeed, I was traveling alone, but I was not alone.

Bus riders were a patient group, as far as action towards station situations was concerned. The bus riders didn't snap back or yell at the offenders. The bus riders didn't challenge the bad guys to fight. The bus riders said nary a word, and if a weirdo was bothering a fellow rider, too bad for that guy.

But I did feel the security of the other passengers if it seemed that something physical was going to happen. I guess part of my realization came from my own feelings. I was sympathetic if a rider was trying to lose someone who was harassing him, but it was his problem. If it looked like it was going to get dangerous, then it was everyone's problem.

We didn't know each other, but we acknowledged a responsibility to take care of each other. I don't think this is the case in other places of society. At a bar, if a fight broke out, I usually just got out of the way. If there was a fight in the street, I would cross over to the other side to avoid getting involved. In bus travel, though, these people were my riding partners. There was a connection. There was a bond. It's hard to explain, but I always felt that if there was trouble, there would be help. If there was a time for action, people would act.

I also noticed that color didn't matter to most of the bus riders. I'm not sure if it is because of where I grew up, but I never trusted black or Hispanic people, and I never felt like they trusted me. I rarely was in situations that required me to trust them, but there was always a sense of discomfort if I had to put my faith in them. I was amazed at how bus riders trusted each other no matter how different they were. I had bonded with people of all colors during this trip, and I had never thought it could be that way.

We weren't in Jackson long before it was time to head to Dallas. After focusing so much attention on X, I was tired and I slept the entire trip to Texas.

I woke up in time to see the sun rising over the huge buildings of the city. I gathered my things and walked out the front door of the Dallas bus station. A friendly cowpoke sauntered up to me.

"Beautiful mornin', isn't it?" he said.

"Why yes, it is." I relished the politeness of the stranger and thought about good old Texan hospitality.

"First time in Dallas?" he inquired.

"Yes, Sir. I'm here for the parade."

"Do you have any dope?" he questioned.

My vision being shattered I said, "Uh, no."

"Do you want to buy any?"

"Uh, no."

"Okay. Have a good one."

And with that he rode off into the horizon, not quite the Lone Ranger I thought he was.

The Super Bowl parade was to start at noon, and at 1:00 p.m. I was to catch a bus to Plano where my relatives lived. The parade was to pass by the bus station, but when I called my Uncle Dick, he suggested that I walk a couple blocks farther down, where the crowd would be throwing confetti from the building tops. I grabbed a bite to eat and then went to secure my place along the street.

People had been lining up early and a crowd had begun to form. I positioned myself across from a big, fancy hotel. I thought I had picked the ideal spot at first, because it seemed to be on the fringe of what could be considered the main section, but before long I realized I was going to be in the heart of the parade route. I noticed that people were moving me to get where they wanted to be. I did little in the way of shoving back, as I knew no one, and if I fell and cut myself, I would bleed Eagle green (and then things would get really ugly).

All this time I wondered where the police were. Eventually they showed up, and brought orange sawhorses with them. These nailed together two-by-fours were supposed to restrain the crowd. I thought it was hilarious, though, since The National Guard couldn't have restrained this crowd. Once the police left, everyone climbed over the sawhorses to get a better spot. I, too, climbed over and was about eight rows deep from the first row, and just in front of the orange barrier.

About an hour before the parade was to begin, cars were still trying to push through the crowd that had swelled into the street. Groups of teenagers were rocking the passing cars and plastering Cowboys bumper stickers everywhere but the bumpers. The chaos started to scare me. Although it seemed good natured enough, I felt that there was a possibility that some of these "pranks" could go too far. But, being from such a small town, I figured I had led such a sheltered life that I didn't know how the big city threw a party.

I remembered back to the parades I had attended in my life. When I was younger, parade day was always a big deal. Since our house was well outside the town limits, it was a chance for me to ride into Strasburg with my parents and then to be free to walk around with my friends who lived in "downtown" Strasburg. People would sit in the lawn chairs that had been lining the street for three days, claiming squatter's rights, preparing for the celebration of the holiday.

We would be a group of eight or nine kids, traveling together, saying "hi" to teachers from school, finding it odd that they were real people with families. We would see our baseball coaches, community leaders, and the pastor of the church all out celebrating whatever holiday it may have been. We even got into some mischief every year at the Halloween parade, where it was customary to throw corn from nearby trees. The leaves that hadn't yet fallen kept us hidden from the eyes of the one cop on duty in Strasburg.

It was different in Dallas, though. There wasn't the peace and excitement I had known in my hometown. It felt dangerous. And though it was a parade, I didn't get that same festive feeling I had known so long ago.

As I stood contemplating the increasingly hostile mass, I was handed a note by a fat man with a beard, who invited me up to his hotel room. After concluding that it wasn't Santa Claus, I respectfully declined. I was to get a lot of practical experience that day.

The parade began as scheduled. I had been waiting on the sidewalk for four hours. I could feel the weight of the crowd pushing at my back, and it was impossible to see anything. On tiptoe, and with my neck completely strained, I could almost make out the players' jerseys. There was quite a battle for position going on in the crowd.

As the cars with the players rolled by, the crowd continually pushed forward. It was too late to enforce the sawhorses as a boundary, so the police came through on horseback and shoved people backwards by running the side of the great beasts into the throng. I couldn't really tell what was going on. I would suddenly feel a surge from the front or the back, and I involuntarily moved with the crowd. I felt like a heifer in a herd of cattle. We were bumping into each other, being prodded by an invisible force.

I started to grow more wary of the goings on around me. I could feel a tension floating through the air as the shoving became more intense. The pressure from the back increased as the big names like Emmitt and Troy by. To add to the chaos, people were standing on the barrier behind me, and when it broke, they fell on those of us standing below them.

As there was one last push forward, and with my nose in the guy's neck in front of me, I felt a something wet on my arm. Immediately, like the front line of the old war fighting style, the first row of people dropped. Women started crying; men were crawling off the street on their hands and knees; parents were scooping up their children in confusion. Then I heard one hysterical woman yell,

"They maced us! I can't believe those #!@*& maced us!"

A feeling of fear and relief ran through me. If the cops were macing the crowd, it must have been getting bad. What would I have done if I was blinded at the moment? I had my stupid duffel bag with me. I didn't know a single soul in the crowd. I would have been a prime target for someone to steal my bag, or worse yet, kick the crap out of me, which I saw happening in isolated incidents around me. I would have guessed that whites would have been the primary targets of these gangs, but it seemed like the blacks were beating each other up at the moment.

I had had enough. I hate the Cowboys. What was I still doing standing there? I began my perilous journey back to the bus station, cursing my Uncle Dick for talking me into walking so far away. This was not going to be an easy task. The exorbitant numbers stretched from buildings into the street.

This was the first mass of people I had ever had to navigate (over 300,000), and I learned that there was usually a single file line of people weaving in and out of the small spaces to make their way through the crowd. In this line, each person put their hand on the person in front of him and there was a hand on his shoulder as well. We were all following a leader we could not see, but we trusted each other to get out of the crowd and into a position of safety. I had my hand on the shoulder of a Spanish guy in front of me, and there was a young black woman with her hand on my shoulder. At one point a fight broke out very near our section of the line, and the young black woman said to me, "Hurry! They're fighting!" I said something like, "I'll protect you," even though I was probably much more scared than she was.

As we moved, it was difficult to see because of the confetti raining down. Black youths were kicking in phone booths and newspaper machines, and I saw kids grabbing stuff off of vendor carts. When I had finally reached the area where the parade had already passed, I moved out to the middle of the street. I seemed to stick out like a sore thumb, but no one paid much attention to me.

Eventually, I was within a half block of the bus station. To my left was a McDonald's and standing in front of it were two black gangs numbering about thirty each, with the gang leaders of each standing face to face. I knew it wouldn't take much for one of them to notice me and call for an all out attack, but both groups had their anger focused on each other. I figured if I got by this, I would be all right.

I moved along quickly, almost on tiptoe. I did not look directly to my left, but I kept the gangs in my peripheral vision. I had bought a Super Bowl banner on a stick, and had broken the stick with hopes that the sheared, pointed end would fend off hundreds of gang members if need be.

Then something happened that gives me shivers to this day.

I moved from the street onto the sidewalk and was about ten yards past the two gangs. I couldn't make out what they were saying to each other, but there was a lot of yelling going on between the two leaders. Suddenly, I heard a loud BANG! At first I didn't know what it was. As I turned around, I saw the one gang leader with a pistol, and there was another loud BANG! and the other leader went down. He had shot him!

I had watched countless movies in my life, and I had seen thousands of people getting shot on television. It's different when it happens in front of you. It was one of the scariest moments of my life. I had imagined myself in this situation so many times. In my dreams, I would jump on the shooter, grab the gun and keep him pinned down until the police arrive.

It didn't work that way. The first thing that went through my head was, "Run for your life, Quay!" And run I did. I had no concern for the fallen "victim." I had no concern for the parents, or children, or the elderly, or anyone else who was on the street that day. I wanted to save myself. And everyone else was doing the same thing. Revelations like these can be sad.

I followed the masses who were screaming and running in the direction of the bus station. The station wasn't very far and I reached it in a short period of time. Unfortunately, it was very difficult to get in, as a large group had gathered around seeking safety. There was nothing but confusion as security at the station would not let people in unless they had a ticket. I, indeed, had one of these precious passes, but was having difficulty getting through the people that had congregated there. I was trying to get my thoughts in order when I saw a young kid pull a gun out and then concealed it again. Again, my chance for heroism was overcome by cowardice, and I hustled away from that spot.

I finally pushed my way into the station and went directly to the front desk. Amid the confusion, I shouted, "When's the Plano bus leaving?"

"Right now! Right now! Get on it! Hurry!" she screamed, probably wishing she could go with me.

I ran, jumped on, and sat as the sweat poured down my face. I hadn't had time to take off my flannel shirt, and it was soaking wet. There was confetti stuck to me and my hands were shaking. I still clung to the broken stick in my hand, which was clenched so tightly, that I wasn't sure I would ever let it go.

Then something strange happened. I started to laugh. Not just a giggle or guffaw, I was laughing outloud. To this day, I'm not sure why. Maybe I was so scared, that I thought it was funny. Maybe I was laughing because the bad guys thought they could get me and I got away. Maybe I just didn't know what else to do. Whatever the reason, I just laughed. And I continued to laugh as the bus ripped out of Dallas, and we left the chaos behind.

It was a completely different scene at the station in Plano. Actually, there was no scene. There was nobody around. Of course, even the Alamo would have seemed peaceful after Dallas.

I called my aunt Joanne from the outside pay phone, then entered the building to wait for her. The station was the smallest I had been to since my journey started, only eight seats or so. The attendant was in the back room and he yelled to me;

"Do you need a ticket?"

"No. I'm just waiting for someone to pick me up."

"O.K. If you don't mind, I'm going to stay back here and watch the Super Bowl parade. It just turned into a riot!"

"No kidding," I mumbled to myself.

5

A week after my narrow escape from death (close enough for me anyway), I was off to Las Vegas, Nevada. I wasn't much of a gambler, but my Uncle Dick glorified the thought of the bright lights, the show girls and how it would fit right into my trip. However, after his suggestion about going downtown for the parade, I wasn't sure I should trust him. Eventually, though, I decided to go. I was headed to Seattle and though Las Vegas was not on the direct path there, it gave the opportunity to put into practice something I learned early in my trip, but had not yet tried.

When I was in Florida, I had inquired about a special Greyhound travel pass that offered unlimited mileage and stops for a month. With the purchase of this ticket, I would need only to flash it as I boarded. Not only would it save me the hassle of waiting in long lines, but it would also be cheaper than continuing to buy tickets from one destination to another.

The Floridian attendant scoffed when I asked him for the pass. "Too much #!@*& money."

I thought he was joking. I had never met a salesman that tried to dissuade me from buying something outrageously priced.

I said, "How much is it?"

"$450. Too much #!@*& money."

I did the math in my head again. At that point I had traveled from Lancaster to Atlanta for $120, and from Atlanta to Port St. Lucie for $80. That's $200 right there and I had been on the road for a total of twelve days. I was going to be buying a ticket to Alabama for another $90, and then another to Dallas, TX for who knows how much, and all of that in the next week. I was convinced that $450 was not an unreasonable price. Confident that this was the right move, I again asked for one of these special passes.

The attendant sighed, looked at me with a fatherly look and said, "Son let me teach you a little trick about bus travel."

Like Ben Kenobi to Luke Skywalker, he spoke of the "force" that would save this young Jedi hundreds of dollars on his trip. Greyhound had some kind of cap on their prices. When I took this trip in 1993 it was $135. What that meant was no matter how far I traveled (one way) the ticket price would not exceed $135. It didn't matter if I was going from Buffalo to Chicago or Boston to Walla-Walla, the price would only go so high.

Now, a bus ticket (which is actually a package of tickets, each one taking me from one city to the next i.e. Lancaster to Harrisburg; Harrisburg to Washington D.C.; and so on) was good for two months from the date of issue. A person could go from one city to the next, spend some time there and then move on when it was convenient, so long as it fell in the two month time frame.

"What if there are cities I want to go to that aren't on that particular route?" I asked Mr. Kenobi.

"Well, Greyhound is somewhat lenient on the routes. They won't let you zigzag up and down all over the country, but they will let you go off the paths if you ask nicely."

From Ben's explanation, it sounded like this was truly the cheapest way to go. I could enjoy the luxury of not waiting in line, plus have the flexibility of a ticket that was good for many places, though not quite all.

When I walked up to Henry, the Greyhound attendant at the Plano station—he had his name on his shirt—, I requested a one way ticket to Seattle that went through Las Vegas. He looked strangely at me and said, "The best connection is through Denver."

I replied, "Yeah, but I'd rather see Las Vegas right now."

"It's going to take you a lot longer through Vegas. Are you sure you want to go that way?" he said politely, but sternly.

"Sure, I'm sure."

His large face at first turned sour. I guess he didn't get many requests for routes that weren't the most efficient. General bus mentality seemed to be, "Get me there as quickly as possible." Actually, that's probably the mentality for most things. I began to worry that he wouldn't do it for me. I was afraid he would refuse the ticket and give me a good talking to about the value of time and efficiency.

The Floridian Jedi appeared to me in an apparition and said, "Use the force, Quay. Use the force."

Henry, oblivious to my mental sighting or the use of my newfound powers, proceeded to punch out the ticket I wanted (actually he said, "Why should I give a #!@*&?"), for the exact total I was told in Florida: $135.

Although Henry probably thought I was a little crazy, he warmed up after the deal was completed. He even offered me a cup of coffee. I watched him move slowly and methodically to the coffee maker. He made me laugh.

He was dressed in a three piece suit, sans the tie. When I looked at him all I could picture was Jeffrey, the butler from *The Fresh Prince*. I guess it was because he went about the upkeep of the station without removing even his jacket. Up the ladder he would go cleaning every light fixture, the dust falling to the floor. Then he fired up the vacuum cleaner. I should mention that he must have had a special liking for *The Price is Right*, because he had the volume cranked up so loud I thought they may have been filming it in his office. I laughed to myself as Henry went about his chores, always keeping one ear tuned into Bob Barker's voice, which resounded throughout the tiny, but tidy station.

There was a good bit of snow falling through the U.S. that year, and the bus we were waiting for had some difficulty somewhere in the north and was already running a good two hours behind schedule. So the four of us, myself, two Mexican passengers, and Jeffrey, went about our business, content to exist in our own little worlds.

Henry had stopped vacuuming and shouted above the sound of the clanging bells and jeering crowd of "The Price" that he would be back in about fifteen minutes.

"All right, Henry. See you in a little bit," I responded.

The Mexicans just smiled and nodded.

As I sat paging through the newspaper it began to dawn on me that he left us here alone with a cash register full of money, not to mention the other wares of the station. I thought about how bizarre it was that he trusted us. Although I had never met a Mexican in my life, I had heard plenty of stories about their criminal activity. I wondered if it was really smart to leave them here in the station unattended, especially with me. What if they don't like hicks?

The two Mexicans sat across from me, and although we were trying not to look at each other, from time to time our eyes would meet. They would occasionally speak Spanish to one another and sometimes it seemed directed at me. I caught a glimpse of myself in a mirror located on the wall of the station. I saw my disheveled appearance: a four day old beard, my stained jeans, my ripped flannel from the riot, my holey boots, and I saw all this behind the frayed bill of my Copenhagen hat. It seemed like they didn't trust me based on my appearance. I imagined what they were saying to each other would sound like this in English:

"Do you theenk Henry should trust heem?"

Although I kept to myself, it pissed me off that these Mexicans seemed to be judging me based on my clothing. They seemed to think I was some sort of criminal just because I might look like "poor white trash." I thought that was completely unfair. Screw them.

Then I caught myself. They were doing the same thing to me that I was doing to them. Judging them based on their nationality, not really knowing anything about them. It was one of those moments when you catch yourself acting like a hypocrite. I decided to ignore them and wait for my bus.

Henry arrived back in the fifteen minutes he had allotted himself and didn't seem surprised in the least that we hadn't moved from our seats. He went and turned the TV down, and it wasn't long before our bus showed up. I bade farewell to Henry whose faith in mankind left an impression in my mind.

Our bus headed back to Dallas. Dallas was the only place to catch a bus going west, so I had little choice in the matter. I was nervous to be going back to the station where so much had happened just a week earlier, but I also realized the circumstances were now quite different.

We made the short trip to Dallas, and I immediately went to my departure exit. The station was busy, but nothing like the last time I had been there. Although it was hot and crowded, I was happy to be getting on the road again. Judging by the tremendous mix of characters waiting alongside of me, it was bound to be a curious ride.

When the bus arrived, I boarded and immediately went and sat in row eight. In my travels, I had realized that where I sat made a difference in the trip. Although the bus functioned as an encasing for a small number of people, within that small world were even smaller subcultures in which similar types of people sat. By the time I had gotten to Dallas, I knew that I could choose a "zone" to occupy depending on my mood.

The back four rows were the "action zone." In this area there were almost guaranteed to be several interesting types of people telling stories, cracking jokes, or being some kind of nuisance. It was generally the most lively section even into the wee hours of the morning. Unlike myself, I don't think most riders made a calculated decision to sit in this "zone." More than likely, their natural character traits drew them there. My theory on this was based on something I observed in high school.

The back provided the area farthest from the only authority figure on the bus, the driver. I know that in my high school you didn't even think of sitting in the back unless you were a jock, a comedian, or a "hoofty." (A "hoofty" was also called a "head," a "hessian" or a variety of other names. They were the people who took ag or shop and usually drove a muscle car after their bus riding days were over.) That logic seemed to have carried over into the "regular" world as I'd be willing to bet that the "action zone" riders had always sat in the back, from their earliest school years to the present.

The front five rows made up the "sleeper zone." This was the area for the quiet people, the people with children, more of the "dorky" characters. These types, too, had probably always sat in this area of the bus. More than likely, they were in band or chorus, the national honor society or the audio visual club. The "sleeper zone" offered safety from the ruffians in the "action zone." Plus, there was the reassurance of the bus driver being close by. This area was the best place to be if you didn't want to be involved in the ruckus. Afterall, have you ever see a fight break out in the front of the bus?

The middle of the bus generally went unnoticed. I was always an "action zone" man in high school, and I could hardly remember who sat in the middle of the bus. That was probably exactly the way those people wanted it. If they felt a need to mingle with either section, they were free to do so. During my travels I had decided that this was the best spot to be.

The area of rows six, seven, and eight was where I usually sat. I called it the "safety zone," because if things got rough in the back I could face forward and ignore it. What I mean by "rough" is arguing, physical confrontations, or boring soliloquies. I saw all these things at different times throughout the trip, and sitting near the back meant there was little chance for escape.

If I sat too far forward, there was a good chance that nobody would want to talk to me for the reasons stated earlier. The people were loner types who often preferred to be left alone. Again, sitting in the front could mean a boring ride without really meeting anyone.

The "safety zone" offered the perfect blend. If I was in the mood to talk, I rarely had trouble finding a conversationalist. If I wanted to keep to myself, I just sat quietly staring out the window.

Usually I chose row eight so I could be right on the fringe of the "action zone," but still able to retreat if I needed to. On any particular trip, at any particular time, these generalizations might have been found differently. But, for the most part, they held true.

I watched from my seat as the strange cast of characters boarded, carefully choosing their "zones" without even knowing it. I was glad that most of them were passing me by, as there were plenty of weirdos in the mix. The bus was nearly full when somebody finally sat with me. He was a middle aged white guy dressed like a bus rider. Basing my judgements on looks, I preferred him sitting with me as opposed to most of the others that had boarded.

"How ya' doin'?" I asked him. I was in the mood to talk and I was eager to make a new friend.

"Fine," he responded.

"Where you headed?"

The standard can't miss.

"Nevada."

And with that one word response, he eased his seat back and closed his eyes. He never said another word the entire trip. I had chosen the correct row, but I had made a seating mistake. When in the mood to talk I almost always sat in the aisle seat. Then, if my riding partner wasn't willing to converse I had the option and freedom of searching for someone who was. It was impossible to talk across a non-sociable partner, and the seats were too high to try and communicate with those in front or behind. I was stuck.

If the riding partner was a talker, it wasn't a big problem being in the window seat. Not only could I talk to him, but he was more likely to search for others from his advantageous seat. But I had screwed myself by not taking into account that this guy might not want to talk to me.

"Do you want to switch seats?" I finally asked him.

He just shook his head. Apparently he liked the aisle seat. I listened with jealousy as lots of stories were being flung around in the "action zone." I wouldn't hear the whole thing, but there would be sudden bursts of laughter to let me know that I was missing out. I tried to stick my head up over the seat, but it was too difficult and uncomfortable. There was a steady flow of banter, and I knew everyone was getting a chance to tell their stories.

About two hours into the trip, though, something opened up, and I had a big decision to make.

One of the primary "movers and shakers" of the "action zone," had a seat open up next to him because his riding partner had gotten off. There was a beautiful seat right next to him, ripe for the taking. But to move from one seat to another without being invited was a bus taboo. As mentioned earlier, the goal of any rider was to secure a pair of seats. It was more comfortable, especially when it was time to sleep. If I had been a boarding passenger at a particular stop, it would have been okay to sit there, but I already had a seat. Now I wanted to move back, depriving him of an empty seat, and I really didn't have a good reason. I thought about it for a little bit, but I also knew that I would have to move without much delay. It would look even worse if I did it further down the line. I hesitated for a moment, then climbed over my sleeping partner.

I plopped down next to the guy and the "action zone" stared at me in disbelief. I had done it. I had deprived this guy of an empty seat. The area was silent as I just sat, facing forward not wanting to piss them off even more. I waited for someone to start screaming at me, but no one said anything.

Everyone just ignored me at first. The conversation picked up again, but I just sat there listening. I was being shunned. Although it made me feel uncomfortable, I still found it better than sitting with that other guy. At least in this spot I could hear the stories. This went on for about an hour, and eventually we had a fifteen minute stop somewhere in the middle of Texas.

I bought a soda and stood by myself, watching in amazement at how well everybody on this bus was getting along. Even the people from the "sleeper zone" were hanging out with each other, telling stories, sharing beverages. It was nice to see, although I wasn't involved in anybody's conversation. Apparently, though, my riding partner had decided that I had paid my dues. As I sipped my Coke, he came up and said, "The name's Kurt."

"Good to meet you, Kurt. I'm Quay."

"Where you from again, Clay?"

"Uh, it's Quay and I'm from Pennsylvania."

"Pennsylvania?! #!@*& worst roads in America, if you ask me. I drive truck, man. I hate going there. Especially Philly. Not only are there potholes, but the streets are too narrow. You try wheelin' a rig around that city."

"Yeah. The roads certainly suck." I responded.

There was an uncomfortable silence and then Kurt finally said it, "I'll tell you what, that was pretty ballsy, what you did on the bus earlier."

"Well. . . I . . . just . . ."

"Now don't get to apologizing like some kind of sissy. I respect you for having the guts to do it. I'm just sayin', I've been riding the bus for a long time, and I've never seen somebody do that. You didn't even ask me! That's my kind of man."

I was glad that he wasn't upset with me, but I started getting paranoid about being his "kind of man." Did he want to date or something? I was always worried about that kind of stuff.

I set my worry aside and chatted with him for the remainder of the break. I knew that things were going to change for me the rest of this trip. Kurt had become a kind of leader in the "action zone," and if he was willing to accept me, then everyone else would as well. Maybe calling him a leader would be a stretch. Basically, he was really funny so most people wanted to be around him. Usually, the person most people want to be around emerges as the leader and I think that was what happened here. Gaining his acceptance was a big step in getting involved in the discussion in the "action zone." I knew that there would be little chance tonight as it was well into the sleep hours, but maybe the next day I would be able to join this happy bus family.

We got back on board. Kurt and everybody else went right to sleep. I did too, satisfied that things were beginning to look up.

Around 3:00 a.m., the bus came to a halt. I awoke from my slumber and looked outside to see a lighted road block that was stopping every car, truck, or bus coming through. Of course, at this time of night, there was almost nobody out.

"What's going on, Kurt?"

Kurt came out of his own groggy state, and squinted his eyes to focus as the inside lights were turned up.

"Ahhhhh, #!@*&. It's the #!@*& border police. They're checkin' for illegal Mexicans."

Three policemen got on and started making their way down the aisle. Every person who looked remotely Hispanic was forced to get out some ID. The guy checking it was pretty rude about the whole thing. He would shine his flashlight into the person's face, ask for identification in Spanish, and then throw it back. He almost seemed upset that everybody was legal.

When he had made his way back to our area, I felt a little nervous. I look more Danish than Mexican, but for some reason I always get nervous in these situations. I remember the first time I crossed into Canada,

"Do you have any firearms?"

"A-h-h-h..n-n-n-o, sir. I-I-I-I d-d-don...."

"Any drugs, alcohol, tobacco?"

"N-n-no. I-I-I-I d-d-d-don...."

"Move along, son."

Here at the illegal immigrant stop, Colonel Klink spared me any embarrassment by passing right over me, but the guy behind me wasn't so lucky. The guy looked Mexican, and the Colonel was giving him a hard time. I wish I could tell you what he was saying, but it was all in Spanish. Finally, the Mexican-looking bus rider spoke up, "Hey, I don't even #!@*& speak Spanish!"

Everybody started laughing except the Colonel.

"Let me see your ID, smart guy!"

The rider checked out, as did everybody else on this ride. The disgruntled Colonel and his two henchmen got off the bus and went back to let us through their roadblock. Kurt encourage all of us to wave as we passed them by, laughing as we did so. Before long it was back to sleep for everybody.

I had slept soundly, and was awakened by a feeling of warmth upon my face. At first I thought I had my head against the heater, but then realized it was the sunrise blazing through the windows. I looked upon a most beautiful scene. We were in New Mexico and the sun was enveloping the wide desert setting, casting shadows on the cacti. The huge rock structures tried to hide the massive glow coming from behind it, but to no avail. This sunrise was inevitable.

People began waking up all around me. I watched as their mouths stood agape at the view. It was times like these that the Greyhound ticket seemed like a bargain. It was about 7:00 a.m. when we stopped for breakfast at McDonald's.

Most everyone was in good spirits this morning. I think it was partially due to the scenery, but I also believed there was a special bond forming among these bus riders. Although I myself had only made friends with Kurt thus far, many of the others were really friendly with each other. This became even more evident when we sat down to eat inside the restaurant.

On every trip to this point, the bus crowd was always scattered throughout the place. Some people sat around the corner. Some people went outside. Some people even got back on the bus. But at this McDonald's and with this group of riders, everyone sat together. There were no cliques. There was no segregation for any reason. Everyone just sat and enjoyed their Egg McMuffins. It was a sight to behold: a busload of strangers now having breakfast as friends.

I had just gotten my order and stood holding my tray,

looking like a freshman in high school cafeteria trying to find a place to sit.

"Yo, Quay! Over here!"

It was Kurt beckoning me to sit with him and the other popular guys from the ride. I made my way over to the table, and Kurt began to introduce me to the knights of this Greyhound roundtable. "Have a seat, Quay. This here is Norman, Todd, and Barry."

I just kind of nodded, smiled, and began pouring maple syrup on my "Big Breakfast."

I examined the physical characteristics of my tablemates.

Barry was a mountain of a man. He appeared to be well into middle age, and his face was worn and unshaven. His entire body was big. Big hands, big head, big chest. He was wearing a sweater, but not one of those sissy L.L. Bean kind. It was similar to one you'd see a lumberjack wearing when he had run out of flannels. His massive hands engulfed the paper cup of coffee which he drank black, of course. I watched as he moved slowly, as if he was just out of energy. He looked to be about as old as my father, but more worn out from life's bad turns.

Todd, on the other hand, was young and wild. He, also, was an enormous man. Atop his huge head was long, blond hair cascading over his broad shoulders, matched with a blond fu-manchu. He wore a sleeveless, black Metallica tee shirt that exposed the numerous tattoos on his arms. On his feet were large, black combat boots. Put all this on his 6'4" frame, and it was pretty menacing.

Norman was the guy who had been given the hard time by the border police. He was much smaller, though not a little guy by any means. He had a number of tattoos as well, but they didn't seem as crude in craftsmanship as Todd's. He had jet black slicked back hair, and a thin, little mustache. He didn't seem as dominating as the other two guys, partly because he was smaller. He was less sure of himself, and he never looked anyone square in the eye. He seemed to be happy just sitting at the table with the rest of us.

And, of course, there was Kurt. At only 5'6" he was definitely the smallest of all of us. He made up for his smallness in stature with a large presence of being. He was cocky and loud, but so funny that we just let him control the conversations and situations. He was in charge.

As for me, I was far from fashionable. In fact, if I had a fashion it was that I had no fashion. Most of my clothes were made of flannel, cotton, jean, or sweat material, and almost all of it had holes in them.

I love baseball hats, and I took three on this trip with me: my extremely beat-up Nike hat, my Copenhagen hat, and a hat with the name of the tree farm where I worked in the winter. By the end of the trip I had lost all of them, but the Nike hat was mailed back to me from South Dakota at some point.

I was about 6 feet, 180 pounds at the time, and kind of dorky looking. I was most often labeled as a "hick," "redneck," or occasionally, "poor, white trash."

"Barry here is from Pennsylvania, Quay, same as you."

"No kidding, Barry? Whereabouts?"

"Philly."

"Philly? Really? What are you doing way out here?"

It was the standard question.

"I'm headed to my parents' place in San Diego," he said sullenly and quietly.

I wasn't sure I should keep pressing. But the bus was about opening up, and if I was going to become a member of this group I had a right to know. Before I could get anything out, though, Barry started in on his story.

"Well, a week ago I found out my wife was cheating on me. I didn't blow up. I didn't hit her. I actually didn't know what to do. I really wanted to kill someone. So before I did anything stupid, I got on the bus that night. Called work the next morning and told them I quit. #!@*& it. I've been on the bus ever since.

Seven #!@*& days."

The words that came out of his mouth were disconcerting, but he didn't really sound sad, just reflective.

"Let me tell you the worst part about it all, Quay."

Wow. I thought. This guy feels really comfortable with me. He is already considering me someone in whom to confide. I leaned a little closer, like a psychologist whose client is about to reveal a dark secret.

"My butt is so sore!"

We all burst out laughing.

It was time to get back on the road.

I sat in the aisle seat right in the heart of the "action zone," looking at all the friendly faces. It didn't take long before Kurt got things started. "All right Pennsylvania Quay. What's your story?"

Curiosity was piqued. I was the new guy, younger than everyone else and had pulled off the bus taboo earlier.

"Well, I'm traveling around America."

Somebody nearby shouted out, "By bus? You're #!@*& crazy!"

When the laughing died down, I tried to explain myself.

"Well, maybe. I've never seen anything, though. I figured the bus would be a good way to see stuff. You know? I come from this small little town. I hadn't seen #!@*&, you know? I hadn't done #!@*&. Now I am. You know what they always say, 'Do it while you're young.' All my buddies are gettin' suit and tie jobs. I'm just not ready yet."

I was spitting it out. I was letting go. And people weren't amazed at my honesty. On the bus you bared your soul.

"Well, where did you get the money?"

"I work in construction and . . .well . . . I just worked until the snow came. Whatever I had in the bank was going toward this trip. I'm just good at saving, I guess. It's a matter of depriving yourself of certain things when you decide what you really want.

My truck is a piece of junk. I live with my parents. I never eat out. But it was all worth it to do this. I can have the other stuff anytime."

Out of respect, the bus was quiet to let all this information sink in. Finally, someone broke the silence. "So where have you been so far?"

As the only one of the bus who was traveling for "fun and adventure," my perspective was unique. I found myself using stories not only to explain where I had been, but also to help me process all that had happened thus far. Writing now in 2006, what I find most interesting about this is that people actually PAY me to tell stories about my adventures. Looking back, much of it began that morning as I explained my life, trip, and thoughts to those people.

I went on to tell story after story. I was on top of the world; the center of attention. It felt so good.

Eventually, I began to feel I was stealing the show and I started to ask questions of others. Todd had been noticeably quiet, and I decided to try and pull him into the conversation. The only thing I knew for sure was that he had to be from New England, due to his thick accent and the fact that he had ordered clam chowder at breakfast.

"Where are you from, Todd?"

"Maine, sort of."

"Sort of? What the #!@*& does that mean?" asked someone else.

His smile, which had been fairly consistent this whole trip faded somewhat. It wasn't as if he was going to cry, but his eyes revealed there was something he didn't want to tell.

"I, uh, just got out of jail in Maine, but I live in Anaheim, sort of. I mean, my parents moved to California when I went to jail, so I'm not from there. But, no it's home, I guess."

This was the first time I had ever been around a guy that had been to prison. I'm not sure what I expected were I ever to meet someone like this, but I was feeling weird. Should I be afraid? Is he some sort of violent monster? Was he a rapist? A pedophile? Thousands of things ran through my mind. There was a dramatic pause in the "action zone."

Kurt was the first to speak up.

"What'd you do, man?"

"Sellin' coke. Five #!@*& years, ya know."

"Ouch. I know the #!@*& feelin'," Kurt lamented. Now our attention was turned to Kurt. What did he mean he knew the feeling?

He had a little smirk on his face when he finally said, "I did three for sellin' coke in Texas when I was younger."

Then Norman jumped in.

"Me too, bro. Three years in Anaheim. Sellin' maryjane, though."

Again a slight hush came across the back of the bus. How many others had done time? I wasn't sure if this was an unusual circumstance, or if I was being naive. Was it typical that several people in any given group had been to jail? I don't think people were shocked or scared. It was just kind of weird. At least to me.

It stayed quiet for a little longer, then Kurt blurted out, "Three hots and a cot! Right boys?!"

Laughter broke up any lingering anxiety, and the guys went into more detail about their crimes and what led up to their arrests. I think it was good for me, because it changed my view of people who had been to jail. In the past, I would have been quick to label a former criminal as a "scumbag" or "worthless." My new friends were not like that, though. Norman and Kurt said that jail straightened them out. It's a hard way to learn, but they did learn.

The discussion moved about once again and I really began to feel close to these riders, especially the guys from the McDonald's table. I had something in common with each of them. Barry was from Pennsylvania, Kurt was a comedian, Norman was a landscaper, and Todd was young (He was only twenty-five and had done five years in prison!). These guys were my friends. My good friends.

As I was laughing over somebody's story about meeting Larry Bird, I realized we were entering a city. For the first time on this trip, I was hoping it wasn't Phoenix. In fact, I was praying it wasn't Phoenix. I was to change connections in Phoenix, and I didn't want this journey to end. I wanted to keep riding with these people. I wanted to take them to Pennsylvania, show them my hometown. I wanted to go with them, see all of America with them. Talk about life and the future and relationships and all those other things philosophers, theologians, sociologists, and educated types think they have a corner on. I wanted Phoenix to be a thousand miles away.

Alas, though, we were there.

I was blue because the whole thing was coming to an end, but I wanted to make sure I had a chance to say good-bye to everybody before going our separate ways. I watched as many members bid adieu to each other, a couple of handshakes, a couple of hugs.

I saw Kurt standing alone, near the telephones.

"Do you have a layover?" I asked him.

"Nope."

"Well, I just wanted to wish you luck with everything. Take it easy. . .whatever."

I kind of wanted to hug him, but that was pretty much out of the question.

"You take it easy, man. Watch out for the bad guys, you know what I mean?"

"Yeah."

There was another dramatic pause, similar to the one when Todd said he just got out of prison. It was really uncomfortable. Maybe this was why riders didn't make a concerted effort to find their new friends before parting ways. It was awkward to say good-bye realizing that I knew him, but I didn't really know him.

More than likely I'd never see him again. But we helped each other get from point A to point B, as had everybody else who had ever been in my life. Whether it was ten minutes or ten years, it didn't take away any importance.

I was startled out of my thoughts when a hand grabbed my shoulder. I turned to find Barry standing there.

"Do you have a layover?"

"Yeah."

"Let's go. I'm buying you a cup of coffee. I need to talk to you. We have to hurry, though, I'm leavin' at two."

He didn't say anything to Kurt, nor Kurt to him.

Apparently, they weren't melodramatic morons like me.

I looked at Kurt.

"Go. Barry knows a lot, so listen to him."

I found Barry sitting at a booth in the station with two, steaming cups of coffee.

"Where are Norman and Todd?" I asked, thinking they were going to join us.

"They're gone," he said, nonchalantly as he blew on his java.

"Gone!?" I said, exasperated, "I didn't even get a chance to say goodbye! What the #!@*&?! Were they in that much of a rush they couldn't stick around two minutes to #!@*& say goodbye?" I should have known better, but I was hurt. Bus schedules are not contingent upon goodbyes. Get on, get off. It's not a movie. One has to make his connection. That said, I still thought it was lousy that they hadn't said goodbye.

Barry stopped me in the middle of my rant. "Quay, this is exactly what I want to talk to you about!"

Hearing him raise his voice this way got my attention. Normally, I would have probably taken offense to it, but Barry had become something of a surrogate father to me on this leg of my journey. He had that tone of voice your dad uses when he is going to tell you something important. As I stood there a bit stunned, he said, "I just want you to sit down and listen to me for a few minutes."

I slowly sat down and put my duffel bag on the seat of the booth next to me. I picked up my coffee and took a sip, although I wasn't looking Barry in the eyes. I felt like a puppy that had just been reprimanded by his owner. Barry finally said, "Look at me." I looked up.

"Listen," he said, "be #!@*& careful out there, man. Know what I mean?"

"Yeah, I gotcha. Be careful."

"No! Listen to me! If you're gonna keep travelin' by yourself, you got to get your #!@*& together!"

Now I was getting angry. I had made it three quarters of the way across the country and had been on the road for a couple of weeks. Did he think I was a little boy?

"I have my #!@*& together!" I retaliated.

"Oh, I know you think you do, but you don't. I'm not going to tell you what to do, but you're a good kid and I don't want to see you getting yourself killed."

Now he had my attention. Killed? I was just riding the bus around the country. Did he really think it could get me killed?

"Look, Quay. It's obvious you're from the country. I mean, even before you told us your story on the bus, it was plain to me that you hadn't been too many places in your life. And that's fine. You can't change that until you've been to some places, right? But there are some things that worry me. You've got to change them, or you're not going to make it much #!@*& further."

His passion led me to believe that I better tune in. "Go ahead," I told him.

"First of all, you've got to cut back on the country-boy act. You've been lucky that you could use it to your advantage in the east and midwest. When you get to Vegas and especially Cali, you're going to become a prime target. There are a lot of #!@*& bad people out there that hang out in bus stations looking for a kid like you. Don't play up the fact that you aren't used to certain things. Pretend like you know exactly what you're doing, even if you have no clue. It will probably be enough to keep certain predators away.

Secondly, you have to change the look in your eyes. You look scared. Bad guys chew up the ones who are scared. You can send a strong message just with the look in your eyes. Walk tall and proud, confident but not arrogant. Send a message to everyone you pass in that station that you are not one to be #!@*& with. Believe it or not, that is usually enough to cause the second tier of bad guys to leave you alone.

Lastly, and this is only for the extreme cases, there will probably be times that the worst of the bad guys will continue to pursue you. There will be moments of sheer anxiety and fear when you know the situation is deteriorating quickly. This is what I want you to do. When the #!@*& hits the fan, when you run into trouble, whatever, just stay cool. Do not panic. If somebody's in your face, don't do nothin'. No one's got your back. Just be cool. Some guy starts #!@*& with you, don't flip out. Just wait. Let it diffuse itself. Usually it will. If it doesn't, it will be time to act. You'll know, because you'll be in #!@*& trouble. You'll be out of alternatives. But don't panic. Wait until you absolutely have to -I can't stress this enough- until there is no choice, then act. Hit hard, hit fast, and get the #!@*& out of there. Don't be afraid to run. Just get the #!@*& out."

These were hard words for me to hear. I thought I was doing just fine in my journey across America. I know I was afraid in many circumstances, especially around the blacks and Hispanics, but I had survived, so I thought I was doing OK. But one thing I have learned about life, probably beginning with this moment in the Phoenix bus station, was to listen to those who are older and wiser. I had thought it was weak to get advice, thinking that some person had something over me. I thought I had to learn everything myself. That couldn't be further from the truth. Any time you can benefit from the mistakes of others, take that opportunity. In fact, one thing I have learned in my advanced age is that even idiots have something to offer. It might simply be how *not* to act in society, but there is always something to learn.

Barry had to catch his bus. He shook my hand like a father parting ways with his college bound son. He had passed down some knowledge that an older, wiser person had given to him years ago. It was out of his hands now. He could only hope that what he taught would be remembered and put into practice.

"Take it easy, Kid," he said, trying not to sound too sentimental.

"Yes, Sir," I replied, the first time I had ever given someone that title.

I sat for another half-hour, but soon it was time for me to leave. I rode by myself in silence as the bus pulled out of Phoenix that afternoon. I was thinking about the things that Barry had said to me. I was going to try and start putting them into practice the remainder of this trip. Right now, though, was a time for sleep, so I assumed my position and fell out of contact with the world.

I awoke to find that it was dark. I sat next to the window staring out into the darkness that had engulfed the desert. As we crested a small hill, I looked ahead to see something utterly amazing. Something that, to this day, I have never forgotten. Sitting smack dab in the middle of the desert were lights. I mean millions of lights. It looked like a spaceship sitting in the distance of the pitch black night. Las Vegas! It was grandiose and glorious, and I could only stare at the incandescent metropolis. From this vantage point it was hard to believe a place like this was called "sin city." It looked alive and happy amongst the dead of night. My excitement grew as we drew nearer to this eternal flame. In thirty minutes we were driving through downtown Las Vegas.

I watched as the big names passed by. Caesar's Palace, The

Mirage, Excalibur, Circus Circus, and Sand's. As I said earlier, I'm not a gambler, but it was special to be in Las Vegas. It was a place where I had to be grown up. A place where I had to be an adult. And I was here alone, free to do anything I felt like doing. It was an amazing feeling of independence.

I spent the night, and most of the next day, wandering around the Strip. As amazing as Vegas first seemed, it began to bore me. For all the differences in the casinos on the outside, the insides were strikingly similar. My bus wasn't scheduled to leave until 10:00 p.m. that night, so I decided to try another trick of bus travel somebody had mentioned to me previously.

In the event I disliked my connection on a certain trip, I had the option of requesting to be rerouted at no extra charge. Since my next connection would take me to Reno, where I would arrive at 5:00 a.m., and have to endure yet another gambling city, I asked to be routed through California, and head north from there. Unfortunately, that bus was leaving in half an hour, which meant I would not have the time to mentally prepare for the ensuing trip. I didn't think it was all that important, so I agreed to have my ticket changed.

Little did I know that this decision would almost cause me to quit the journey.

6

I now sat in the Las Vegas terminal knowing that my bus would be arriving soon. It was difficult to set my mind on the fact that I was going to be leaving in a matter of minutes instead of the six hours on my original ticket. In general, I usually got to the station one to two hours ahead of time in order to get information, write in my journal, and get my mind prepared for the long, upcoming journey. Though I felt a little bothered by the whole thing, I figured I'd get over it once we started moving.

I was rushing around to get my stuff together and secure a spot in line, when I noticed a relatively attractive older lady sitting in the same line with me. She looked about thirty-five, and she sat upright in her seat, her legs crossed, and a pair of little glasses perched on the end of her nose. She was dressed casually —jeans, sweatshirt, Reeboks— but for some reason I guessed she was a middle class type. With her face buried in a book of Shakespeare, she seemed to be posing as an intellectual.

Having a degree in English and loving Shakespeare, I figured I knew enough about the Bard to carry on a decent conversation. I took a couple of minutes to recollect as many of his plays as possible, but before I had mustered up enough nerve to talk to her, our bus had arrived.

I was in the middle of the boarding line, and once on the bus, I chose row nine, mainly because everything else was filled. I saw my Juliet wandering up the aisle. She was encountering many people practicing *dpm*. If the others were as smart as me they would have counted the number of people in line. It was going to be a full bus, so it was better to try and find someone preferable with whom to sit.

In this case that person was Juliet. And I her Romeo.

"Excuse me miss, would you like to sit with me?"

"Why, thank you!" she said in an overly gracious tone

which meant she really didn't want to or she was an overly gracious person.

"Where are you headed?" she asked.

"Well, I'm going to Seattle. Eventually. But I switch buses in Barstow," I replied.

"I'm going to Barstow, too! Again, thank you soooo much for letting me sit here," she said, her voice still excited.

"No problem," I said, feeling like I had donated a kidney rather than a seat.

The bus started to pull out and before long we were on the Strip headed out of town. On the way we passed the Excalibur hotel, a grand spectacle with its castle-like architecture and medieval theme. Just a skosh more grandiose than the Hotel Nevada and Casino where I had slept for $35.

"That's where I stayed last night," Juliet announced.

"Wow! Really? How did you like it?"

"I found it funny how so many of the allusions there didn't even coincide with Arthurian legend! There were certain items that one wouldn't even find in the same century, let alone King Arthur's court."

"Yeah. I don't think they had slot machines and crap tables back then."

I thought it was funny.

The unamused Juliet continued.

"For example, those horses? In King Arthur's time they wouldn't be . . ."

She went on to tell me something about the horses that only an expert would know. Not only that, but she went on to point out at least three other "glaring" inaccuracies on the outside of the building alone. Now, I'm all for "authenticity," but the bottom line? This was Vegas. The inside of almost all these buildings are the same: thousands and thousands of one armed bandits and thousands and thousands of people who believe in "luck." It's all a big, phony pageant. If I thought for a second that the majority of people were more concerned about the building than with the possibility of winning money, I'd be on her side. But people don't come to Vegas for lessons in history or literature. They come to throw away good money.

We sat quietly for a spell, as the bus roared through the desert. I decided that maybe I would try a different approach. I've always been curious about the sports teams people root for. In Lancaster, we're close enough to Philadelphia that the majority of people cheer for the Flyers, Sixers, Eagles, and Phillies. We are blessed to have four major sports within easy driving distance. Plus, Baltimore, Washington D.C., and Pittsburgh are not too far away, so there are a slew of teams that one could follow and have the opportunity to see. I just like to know which teams the locals support.

Juliet was from Southern California, and at the time of this trip three teams, the Rams, Chargers, and Raiders, all hailed from the area. I thought this would be a safe topic to throw out.

"Who do you root for in football?" I finally asked.

"Football? Are you kidding? I don't watch football. I think it's a barbaric sport, played and watched by barbarians."

"Sorry. Me not know you feel that way," Conan replied.

"Really all sports are for kids. It's unbelievable that they pay these athletes an exorbitant amount of money, and the ignorant masses with nothing going on in their lives go out and consistently support them. Of course, I guess if that's all you have, what else are you going to do?"

Well, I had missed again. I guess it wasn't the best of topics to attempt, but I didn't realize her feelings would be so strong. I would have to be more careful to pick topics that weren't so controversial. . . wait a second . . . football? It wasn't that controversial, was it? Be that as it may, I knew I'd better watch my tongue.

Just to talk, as opposed to trying to start a conversation, I spoke up again.

"Man, I'm starvin'. I hope we stop soon. I could use a Big Mac or something!"

"Oh, feasting on the flesh of another living thing! That's so disgusting! It makes me shiver. I've packed my own hummus sandwiches, so I don't care where we stop."

I didn't have the heart to tell her that a Big Mac probably had about one percent "flesh" in it. And, by the way, what in the world is hummus?

I decided to keep quiet. If she was going to have something negative to say about everything I brought up, then it wasn't worth it. Besides, it really felt like she was talking down to me, and I can't stand that.

I remained to myself for about an hour, but I didn't enjoy doing it. I shouldn't have been discouraged just because somebody was a little condescending. Instead, I should want to try and make it right. I had forgotten about our Shakespeare connection, and I decided to give it a shot.

"I saw you were reading some Shakespeare. Are you a big fan?" A little startled she said, "Why, yes. You like Shakespeare?"

"Yeah. In college I read about fourteen of his plays."

She was taken aback. It was like she was impressed that I was smart enough to read, let alone to know anything about William himself. Her eyes were saying, "This meat-eating, football-loving, tractor-pulling Redneck reads Shakespeare?"

The conversation took off from there and we had an intelligent discussion on theme, symbolism, denouement, and all that other crap that only English people enjoy. But the whole conversation was somewhat tainted for me knowing she looked down on me until she started seeing me as an equal. In my mind I cursed her. How dare she think of me as below her? Even if I hadn't known anything about Shakespeare there would be no reason for her to treat me like a second rate human, football fan or not. By doing it she was telling me that my differing ideas, differing prerogatives, differing interests, were not as important as her own.

How dare she!

As I ranted against this woman in my head, another thought came to mind. I asked myself, "How often do you judge people before you know them? How often do you treat people differently because of their skin color, clothing, beliefs, and interests? It was another one of those times when you catch yourself doing the same things for which you were criticizing someone else. Doesn't it suck when you find yourself doing that?

Juliet and I both had layovers in Barstow, but we talked very little when we got there. I nursed a Dr. Pepper and stared into the night. I felt odd here. I didn't know any of my connection times, only the cities where I was to change. I usually had my connection sites and times memorized, always knowing where I would be at any given time of the day. Sometimes the buses fell behind, but I always had an idea of when and where we were due during the day. By getting my ticket changed, and our immediate departure, I knew only the direction I was going. How long from city to city? I didn't know. Long layovers? I didn't know.

I parted ways with Juliet here.

"It was good talking to you," I lied.

"Alas, poor Yorick. I knew thee well," was her stupid reply.

I boarded and sat in row eight for no reason other than it was my favorite spot. There weren't many people riding, and it was nighttime anyway, which generally meant sleeping. It would have required me to go out of my way to meet anybody, and I was tired to do anything. I'd only slept for about three hours at the hotel in Vegas, and after running around for the day, I had ridden the bus with a pompous blowhard to this point. I just wanted to sleep.

And sleep I did, like a baby after feeding time.

Around 6:00 a.m., I woke up to a clear sunny day and was informed that we were two hours from Sacramento. I knew I had to change buses there, but I had no idea what time I was to catch my bus to Oregon. Was there a layover? And when I got to

Portland was there a layover for Seattle there? Normally, I would have tried to talk to a ticket agent and find out exactly where I was going, but I just didn't have time at any of the stops. For the first time on the big trip I was completely clueless.

It was also adventurous. A man and his bag, not knowing times or schedules. Like a leaf in the wind, a stick in the stream, or any other corny metaphor you want to insert, I was floating across California on the Greyhound. The Jack Kerouac for Generation X, as one of my friends called me (even though I can't stand Jack Kerouac).

There was little time between my arrival and subsequent departure from Sacramento. We had gotten there at 7:50 a.m., and were off to Portland at 8:00 a.m. In my bliss of ignorance, imagining myself a sparrow searching for a tree limb, I said to the driver as I boarded my new bus;

"What time are we due in Portland tonight? Six? Seven?"

He had a look on his face like that of a person who had been asked how much something cost and relished the fact that the price was going to be way more than the questioner had anticipated.

"Try midnight."

After picking my jaw up off the floor I said, "Are you sure?" He shot me a different look this time, more like, "I drive this route everyday, you idiot! Of course I'm sure." But a simple "yes" was his response.

If we only got to Portland at midnight, how long before my bus would leave for Seattle? And if I was so wrong in guessing the time getting to Portland, maybe it would take days to get there. Maybe it was on the other side of the world! No wonder Kerouac did drugs all the time.

This event gave me a new perspective on time. I found schedules necessary to grasp the concept of time and to make the most of it. Without an idea of what time it was, I was spending a lot of it wishing I was somewhere else. The vision of living life without a watch and a calendar is romantic, but I like to see things with a beginning and an end so I can make the most of what's in between.

I wandered back the aisle, dazed and disillusioned, only to find that there was only one spot left, and that was the very back seat. This seat had its good and bad points. It actually seated three, so if there were only one or two people, it offered more room than the standard pair. The problem was, if there was a full bus, there were three people jammed into this spot. It quickly went from being the "best" seat in the house to the worst, especially if you became the middleman in a stranger sandwich. The back seat was also right beside the bathroom which needs no explanation. It was as deep into the "action zone" as a rider could get. If things got bad, there was no escape.

I approached the seat and asked, "Is it all right if I sit here?" It was really a dumb question because there weren't any other seats, but it was still polite to ask.

"Sure."

I sat down and pretended to be shifting things and looking at some papers, so I could examine my riding partner. He had neatly cropped blond hair, the front of which was beginning to thin out. He was quite young looking, and I figured he was a businessman of some sort. I've always found it was easy to spot a businessman because they are so used to wearing jackets and ties that they make jeans, sweats, and tee shirts look uncomfortable. They keep the shirt tucked in, never go without a belt, and their sneakers are always cottonball white from lack of use.

I cursed my luck because I generally don't get along with business types. I again caught myself making a generalization similar to the one Juliet had made about me. I think it was a little different, though, because it wasn't a matter of superiority. It was just about dissimilar interests. Anyway, I was ready to try to tackle the tough world of business jargon like "debit" and "spreadsheet." We sat silently for about fifteen minutes, while he finished sizing me up himself. He finally spoke up.

"Well, where ya' headed?"

"Seattle. How 'bout yourself?" I replied.

"Well, back to Spokane. But I'll be moving to Sacramento in the next two weeks. You from there?"

"No. No. I'm from Pennsylvania. The name is Quay."

"Glad to meet you, Clay. I'm Scott."

And the friendship was on.

Scott was being relocated to Sacramento from his job in Spokane. He was indeed a businessman in the capacity of a manager/salesman. He spoke of his job as a job; the money was good, he got to travel some, but it wasn't really fulfilling.

I asked him the question I ask anybody who dislikes their job, "Why don't you just quit? I don't understand."

"I'm too far gone now. I'm thirty-four years old, and I've been with this company for eleven years. I make good money for a guy my age. I can't just up and quit. We're not all lucky like you. Able to travel around and all."

I took some offense at this. I was not lucky. I planned my trip. I worked hard to make the money to take this trip. I intentionally avoided getting a "career" job, which would have compounded the problems when ready to travel. I was smart if anything. But I still don't see the sense in holding onto a job where you are not being fulfilled. I really don't see any sense in doing anything that isn't fulfilling.

I wasn't mad at Scott, but when I talk to guys like him it reaffirms the way I handle things. There is a lifetime of things to do and I guarantee I won't waste my time wishing away days at a job I dislike.

"Well, I wasn't really lucky. I . . ."

"I'm sorry, I don't mean lucky. I mean. . .I just. . .I guess I'm just envious. You know? But I like my life, too. I'm engaged to a beautiful woman, and I love her so much. She's actually pretty excited about moving down to California. She and I grew up in Spokane, so it will be good for us to get out of there. I'm sure you understand how much you can learn just getting away from your roots."

Did I ever.

As Scott and I talked, I could feel my stomach beginning to growl. I hadn't eaten anything substantial since the day before, and my diet of Snickers and Coke was starting to wear thin. Our bus was running a little late, and they wanted to try to keep everyone's connections intact, which was fine with me. I surely didn't want to miss mine in Portland.

It had begun to rain and I was confused where we were. All I knew for sure was that we were somewhere north of Sacramento, CA and south of Medford, OR, two places I would never be able to identify on a map. I was also starving, which wasn't helping my discomfort. Finally, a good two hours into the trip, we stopped to get something to eat. I ran to a little Mexican joint at the corner of a small shopping complex. I wasn't a big fan of Mexican food, but I didn't see any other places around.

"Give me two burritos, please."

As I was waiting for my food, I found it strange that no one else was getting anything to eat. Usually it was a mob scene when the bus unloaded so I thought maybe I missed an announced lunch time which was near at hand. Whatever was going on, I was starving and I was going to eat. I was sure I could force down some more food in an hour or two.

After the fifteen minute break (which was fourteen minutes longer than it took me to eat my burritos), we got back on board to continue our journey. It was raining even harder and most of the people on the bus had that comfortable feeling you get as you lie in your bed on a dreary Saturday morning. Nothing to do. Nowhere to go. It's perfect for sleep. The bus was peaceful and quiet, and Scott had drifted off, so I decided to do some journal writing.

As I scribbled down some ideas, I felt a new grumbling in my belly, but it was no longer hunger induced. I tried to ignore it, but the small explosions spread from my stomach to all parts of my body. The pressure would finally find a release nozzle, and the discharge would make its way into the stale bus air. What was going on here? It felt like the whole seat was shaking! Was I the only one feeling this?! I put my journal away and shut my eyes trying to fool it into thinking it was time for rest, but a stomach never falls for that one. It just grumbled louder, insisting that I take care of it.

The small gurgles gradually grew larger, and I could almost feel the formation of each bubble, building and growing, floating throughout my body, angry as it searched for a point of release. The more I fought it, the greater the pain and the louder it got. I felt like a shook up bottle of soda waiting for the cap to be removed so I could explode. I was beginning to realize why so many had passed on the Mexican food at our last stop.

The bathroom was right next to me, but the thought of sitting on a moving target that had been shared by some of the buttocks on this bus caused me to think again. I was glad that Scott was sleeping because he may have been offended by some of the noises that came from me that afternoon. I was fortunate, though, as a stop was due in a few minutes and when we arrived, I had already gotten to the front of the bus before the driver even shifted into second.

I was standing on the steps when the door opened, and like a shot from a cannon, I was in that station bathroom so quickly, not even one drop of the central California rain hit me in my mad dash to relief.

Although I felt much better as we continued in our trek north, the weather got worse and worse as our elevation increased. The air was considerably colder and the rain had turned to snow. Not nice, white, flaky, "it's-beginning-to-look-like-Christmas" snow, but wet, disgusting slush. This kind of weather made for miserable riding. The bus had to travel slowly and it was much too snowy to see any scenery.

The weather had a bad effect on the bus itself, but it did even more damage to the riders. I had mentioned earlier the wonderful "rainy Saturday" feeling. It wasn't morning anymore, and after six hours it felt less like being under the covers and more like being in a coffin.

Even with the misery of the ride, I was glad to be riding with Scott. In a lot of ways I think we were keeping each other sane. He was pretty cool, as far as businessmen go, and I think he liked me (as far as idiots go).

"You know I really admire what you're doing, Quay."

"What do you mean?"

"Well, you're doing it. You're seeing the country. Lots of people talk about it, probably everybody at one time or another but they just never do it."

"Yeah, well, I just don't understand why people feel the need to just take a job they hate and then work the rest of their lives at it." I think my ego fueled me when he complimented me for taking this trip.

"But, Quay, you have to think about other people and their lives. Not everyone planned things out as well as you. People have college debts, credit cards, vehicles, and so on. You made good decisions to prepare yourself for the opportunity and then you followed through."

"Well, then they shouldn't have made mistakes."

"Quay, don't you make mistakes? Didn't you get a lot of breaks that helped you get where you are? Aren't you lucky to have had parents that helped you out for half of your college expenses? Isn't it convenient that your parents let you live at their house after you graduated from college? You can't blame people for not having the breaks that you had."

"Well, maybe. But that still doesn't excuse people for working at a job they find unfulfilling. Why would you spend day after day working at a job you hate? That doesn't make any sense to me."

"Let me ask you this question. Do you have more respect for the guy who quits a job he hates, but then is unable to feed his family. Or the guy who guts it out day after day to make sure his family not only survives, but thrives?"

This caused me to reflect. "I guess I never thought about it that way."

Scott continued. "In a perfect world, every person would have a job he loves, make plenty of money, and enjoy life every single day. That isn't reality, though. And the bottom line is that family is more important than your personal happiness. That's not giving up. That's not weak. That's maturity."

Maybe I was a little hard on people. I've always been a driven person, and I pursue my dreams, sometimes with reckless abandon. But that is easy to do if I only have to answer to myself. What would I do in other circumstances? I realized that I needed to reflect on other people and their lives. It was easy to criticize and condemn when I had never even taken the time to think about their position. I needed to start doing that more often. It really changes your perspective.

The travelers had grown restless. It had been forever since we had stopped, and we were all getting buggy staring at the falling slop. Finally, in a place called Weed, CA, the bus came to a rest.

All of us moved slowly off the hot, smelly bus, and into the freezing wet rain/snow. We wandered aimlessly, one behind the other, searching for the station. Strange as it may seem, we couldn't seem to locate it. There were no buildings resembling a station: a place with hot food and a decent bathroom, a place to buy some supplies, a place to play some Pac-Man or something. Anything.

Someone called out to the driver, "Where the #!@*& is the station?"

"Right there! Where did you think it would be?" He pointed his finger towards a building that resembled a shed more than a place of of business. There was a communal groan and we moved forward, trying to get out of the rain. We did our best to cram ourselves into the small, dark building. It seemed like the place was run as a mom-and-pop deal, and though friendly, I felt like telling them they should think about expansion. I started to look through the wares that were for sale. Of course, it was a bunch of crap with "Weed, CA" stamped somewhere on the item. It made me feel a little at home, because they do the same thing in Lancaster. You'll see some rock that says, "Amish country. Lancaster, PA." Just a bunch of junk. I mulled over a handsome "Weed, CA" tee shirt for one of my hippie friends, before deciding that I'd rather spend my $10 on soda, crackers, and candy bars in case I never had another opportunity to eat in my life.

At first, I stayed inside the building, standing with candy under my arm, spilling soda all over myself because every time someone so much as scratched his armpit, it caused a chain reaction of people bumping into each other. It was so small I felt like getting back on the bus just to have more room. Soon I had to get some air. Apparently somebody else had eaten the wrong thing and the environment in the shack was stifling. I tried to stay dry under the small overhang of the building, but still ended up with a good soaking.

"All right people! Let's get loaded up!"

The driver was beckoning the crowd back to the bus. I was a bit torn. I was drenched and freezing, so it would be nice to go back to the warmth. But then I remembered that the warmth was a busload of people and we had at least another eight hours to ride. That was if nothing went wrong. And then those eight hours only meant I was in Portland. Who knew how many more to Seattle? I remembered how I didn't want the trip to Phoenix to end with my new-found buddies, and how I would now probably give up my life just to *not* get back on that bus. I didn't want to get on that freakin' bus. I wanted to be in Seattle. Moments like these play tricks on your mind.

The crowd slowly made their way to the bus, like a herd of

steer headed to slaughter.

It was still snowing when we crossed the border into Oregon. Night had fallen, and despite the fact that the heat was cranked up, we were all chilled with dampness from our stop in Weed. Discomfort loomed as there was no escape from the squeaking of the wet shoes on the rubber floor, the smell of stale sweatshirts, and the ever falling slush around us. It was like an ominous Twilight Zone as we crawled up Route 5, and I waited for us to drive off a cliff, or find ourselves in a foreign country.

Our first stop in Oregon was Ashland, where we were greeted by twenty-five people standing in an orderly line, soaked and freezing. The Ashland station closed at 5:00 p.m. and since we were running an hour behind, they were forced to wait outside when closing time had come and gone. The people were lined up along the edge of the building hoping that the overhead rainspout would be enough to keep them dry. Apparently not. This station was off the beaten path, and there was one solitary light hanging on the edge of the roof. Otherwise, it was black.

I could see their faces as we pulled in. It was outright sorrow. For the first time in this leg of the journey I actually felt happier being on the bus than off it.

This was a scheduled smoke stop (There was no smoking on the bus, so five minute stops were scheduled for people who just couldn't go two hours without a cigarette. The stops were much more frequent when the driver was a smoker.) I hadn't talked to my aunt in Seattle since leaving Las Vegas and she was anticipating my arrival. I decided to use this stop to try to get in touch with her. There was an outdoor pay phone below the one security light, which was next to the passengers who were waiting to board. I should mention that these people were forced to continue standing in the freezing rain until the smoke break was over.

I wanted to talk to my aunt just to hear a familiar voice. I wanted her to offer me words of encouragement or something. I wanted her to say, "hang in there" or some other overused cliché. I needed to talk to some family. I needed a pep talk.

I was getting a good soaking of my own waiting for the collect call to go through. Finally, the operator made the connection with Aunt Norma.

"Hi Quay. Where are you? We'll come get you."

"I'm not in Seattle, yet, Norn. I'm in Ashland."

"Ashland, Oregon?! When are you supposed to get here?!"

"I'm not sure."

She paused a moment, then said, "Well why'd you call?"

Standing in the rain, soaked to the bone, feeling sick to my stomach and like I was going to cry, I hesitated and then said, "I'm not sure."

"Just call me when you get here. Bye."

Norma was always thrifty, so she was probably a little pissed that I wasted a collect call to tell her nothing. So much for my words of encouragement.

Gotta love family, huh?

By the time I had finished my twenty second phone call, it was time to reboard. Unfortunately, more people were getting on then were getting off. This posed a problem. Usual Greyhound policy was that everyone had to have a seat. If seats weren't available, those unlucky people would have to wait until another bus stopped that was going in that direction.

In this case, I had hoped they would make an exception. Sure, it would be more uncomfortable for everyone, but it would be inhuman to leave anybody for another few hours in the harsh Oregon elements.

"Just find a place to sit," was the order from the driver.

Scott and I knew we were going to receive a riding "third," and it was just a matter of time until someone saw the opening in the back. I had hoped it would be a beautiful blond with a cheesesteak, but instead it was a short, chubby lady with a huge bag. We now formed the stranger sandwich I had talked about earlier, with me as the lunchmeat. Every seat was full and there were four riders sitting on the muddy floor. Also, with the overhead compartments at maximum capacity, there were handbags, backpacks, guitars, and anything else one could imagine jamming up the aisle.

The driver addressed the crowd.

"Now everybody is going to have to be patient with each other. There are a lot of people and I know everybody is frustrated. Just hang in there."

Well, my aunt didn't say it, but the bus driver did. I just had to hang in there.

There was a strange looking guy who got on and sat right in front of us. He had his cap pulled down over his eyes, with the tufts of his pork chop sideburns sticking out the corners. Everything he wore was black. Black tee shirt, black jeans, black combat boots. Of course he had one of those stupid chains hooked onto his wallet. He wasn't muscular or anything, but his all black gear, quiet demeanor, and look of demonic possession made him seem intimidating.

He had carried a briefcase with him, and once on the road he opened it and produced a tape recorder. I wasn't sure what he intended to do with this, since playing a tape recorder without headphones was against the rules. Well, he hit play anyway and a funky, slow, hip-hoppish love song came on. I thought "Oh, great, now I have to listen to this crap." He had it turned down low, but everybody in the back could hear it. I'm positive the driver couldn't because he would have made him turn it off immediately.

We listened, and when the song was over I figured that was the end of it. But no sooner did it end than the song came on again. The same song! I figured he was lonely and this was his and his girlfriend's "song." Maybe he just liked it. I don't know, but it was weird.

In a muffled voice, I leaned over and said to Scott, "What's going on? Is that the same song?"

"I think so," he replied very hushed, so as not to anger the Demonic Song Player.

After the song ended the second time, we sat there, just waiting to see what would happen next. And the same song came on again. And then again. And then once again. And another time. I kept a tally of the number and he went on to play the song fifteen consecutive times! It wasn't like he was listening to the song, rewinding, and listening to it again. He had it taped fifteen times in a row on the cassette! With the short lull between each song, we would all look at each other in anticipation that this would be the last time. It would be deathly silent, and then the slow beats on the recorder would start up again causing a communal groan that everyone, except Demonic Song Player, heard. Then again, maybe he did hear, but didn't care.

No one said anything, I guess because everyone was afraid or thought it rude to tell him to stop (As if someone who played the same song fifteen consecutive times was going to be concerned with etiquette.). Looking back, I wish I would have said something. I wish I would have blurted out, "Shut that #!@*& thing off you idiot!" Maybe I would have gotten lucky and he would have killed me and put me out of my misery.

Relief was promised in the city of Eugene. Apparently there were supposed to be seventeen people getting off there. That was true. But waiting in line at the station were thirty more people intent on getting to Portland themselves. The station here was still open, though, so once we were full, the rest were going to have to wait for the next bus. Actually, the passenger turnover was for the better. Five extremely drunk, obnoxious teenagers got off, plus Demonic Song Player, and the chubby lady who was sitting with us.

We watched as the new riders boarded. Coming up the aisle was a guy with long braided hair and a matching braided beard that hung halfway down his chest. He had on knickers and rainbow suspenders, just like the ones Mork used to wear. It was the first time I ever saw anyone wearing knickers other than on Halloween. I was hoping he wouldn't sit with us. Hippies and country folk just don't get along. Especially middle aged hippies. My dad fought in Vietnam. This guy was probably some draft-dodging, pinko, commie, liberal in my book.

So, of course, he sat with us.

The first thing he did when he sat down was introduce himself. "Hi guys. The name's Michael."

"Oh, great," I thought, "he's a peacenik. Wants to be buddies with everybody."

Scott wasn't as nearly judgmental as I, and he said, "How are you doing Michael. My name is Scott and this is Quay."

"Glad to meet you both," he said with his toothy, PETA, tree-hugging smile.

I was apprehensive about taking the discussion any further. I didn't want to get into some highly politicized conversation that would cause me to beat the crap out of him. I was frustrated with this whole leg of the journey, and I knew it wasn't going to take much to set me off. Michael wanted to talk, though.

"Sometimes bus travel sucks, doesn't it?"

Scott and I both nodded our head in affirmation, but didn't really say anything. Michael continued.

"I remember traveling around America in the 70s by Greyhound. It was even crazier back then. People would get really drunk and cause a lot of commotion. There were fights, buses would break down, lots of problems. Believe it or not, the service has actually gotten better since then."

I couldn't resist.

"Did you take the trip after your tour in Vietnam?"

Michael started to laugh. I thought, "Here it comes! Let's go Hippie boy!"

"I guess the gray hairs in my beard make me appear older than I really am. I didn't turn 18 until 1975, and the war was over by then. I took the bus trip about a year after graduating from high school."

I felt stupid. I guess I am stupid. Feeling dejected that I wasn't going to be able to defend my radical right-wing position, I decided to just make conversation. "Why did you take off on a trip after graduation?" I inquired.

"Well, I wasn't sure what I wanted to do for a 'career.' My parents and a lot of people were on my back about college, my job, my future. I wanted to see America before I did anything else. So, I left. I spent four months seeing the country. Best thing I ever did."

I replied, "That's kind of what I'm doing."

"That's cool, Quay. We're probably a lot alike. Tell me some of your stories." That scared me. Me? Like a hippie? What was going on in my life? I hated hippies more than I hated blacks, and now I was having a hard time hating this guy. Not only that, but we're alike!? This was too much.

Michael and I swapped stories for an hour or so, and eventually he wanted to sleep. Scott was already asleep, so I was left alone to my thoughts as I sat between the two.

I wondered how I could have something in common with a guy like Michael. I mean, in our discussion and our stories I found that he and I were very similar in how we felt about many things, including politics. But, how could somebody that looked like that have anything in common with me? Maybe there is more to a person than their clothes.

In fact, I was sitting between two people at that moment that had proven my stereotypes incorrect. Scott was a businessman, yet we got along great. I don't know how I would have made it without him thus far. Michael would be labeled a "hippie," yet he didn't match every characteristic that goes with the label. I started questioning whether or not it was prudent to figure out who people are before ever having met them.

It also took me back to Juliet with whom I had ridden at the beginning of this trip. It was obvious that she had been judging me based on my clothing. I was probably the first "redneck" she ever met that knew anything about Shakespeare. I remembered how much it pissed me off that she measured me that way. Yet, sitting here, I realized that I do the same thing with people all the time. Why should I be surprised at how well I was getting along with Scott and Michael? We're all more than just our clothing, aren't we?

We reached Salem just before midnight. Michael got off, and I was glad that I got to know him. I wondered how many times in my life I had shunned people who would have been a great blessing to me. Anyway, the driver made an announcement that Portland was a short hour up the road. The nightmare was almost over! As I started to breathe easier, knowing that this all would be coming to an end soon, I saw a short but rotund shape coming back towards us. There were a number of seats open so I wasn't too worried about gaining an occupant, but this guy was staggering up the aisle and I wondered what his story was and how close he was going to be sitting to us.

He seemed to be looking for a spot by bumping his rear end against the aisle seat, and if someone pushed him, it meant that it was taken. It was almost as if he were blind. Finally, in the seat directly in front of us, he went to bump, found no push, and to the chagrin of the guy in the window seat, he plopped his meatball frame into the seat.

He was an old American Indian and he was blind, all right. Blind drunk. At first he mumbled in a language no one knew, barely audible. And then with his finger, he began to poke the guy he was sitting with.

"Don't!" the passenger said, in a little sissy voice.

The Indian paid no attention, and poked him again. I don't know exactly what he was doing, but I felt for Sissy Guy. He was the guy that had to sit with Demonic Song Player, and now he was stuck with Drank 2 Much.

"Don't!" he said again. Then he turned around.

"Could I please come back with you guys?"

"Of course. Of course." I didn't necessarily want to be in a sandwich again, but we riders had to take care of each other.

Drank 2 Much swayed in his seat for a little and then noticed the small Mexican guy laying in the aisle. It wasn't uncommon on late night bus trips to see people sprawled out on the floor trying to get some sleep. Drank 2 Much reached over and poked the Mexican in the back, and the Mexican came up swearing (I guess he was swearing. It was in Spanish, so I can't say for sure.). He laid back down, and Drank 2 Much poked him again. This time he sat up and I know he was swearing. "Knock it the #!@*& off, you #!@*&!" he yelled in English.

The three of us looked at each other, but didn't say a word. It had been a long, horrible trip, and this was the icing on the cake. We watched as the poking and the swearing went on for a while longer until, finally, Drank 2 Much became Sleep So Long.

Sissy Guy shared this:

"I've been riding the bus every week for thirteen years. This is, hands down, the worst trip I've ever taken."

We rolled into Portland at 1:00 a.m.. We were an hour late, but they had been kind enough to hold the bus for Seattle. Scott and I boarded, and though there was a chance we could have gotten our own seats, we decided to sit together and avoid any further hassles.

We didn't say a word to each other and were asleep within fifty seconds of pulling out of Portland. It was just sheer exhaustion. We had been fighting the cold, the snow and the crazy people for the last sixteen hours and it was soon going to be over.

I slept like a rock, and the next thing I knew we were in Seattle. It was around 6:00 in the morning.

Scott was headed out the door because his ride was already waiting. "Take it easy, Scott. That ride really sucked."

"Yeah it did. See ya'."

I went and found a phone and called my aunt. This time I used a quarter.

"Norma. It's Quay. I'm in Seattle. I hung in there."

7

My aunt and uncle picked me up and had me at their house, sucking down some coffee. They were throwing out questions.

"What was your favorite place?"

"Did you meet any interesting people?"

"How much money do you have left?"

I did my best to answer each one without sounding like an ingrate, but I was tired.

"Where are you going next?"

That question, though, stopped me mid-blueberry muffin.

Where *was* I going next? My first thought was to fly home. I had made it across America and I was sick of the bus. I was tired of its inefficiency. I was tired of eating nothing but fast food. I was tired of the way it crept from place to place, always crowded and uncomfortable. The thought of going anywhere else in that eight-wheeled prison was something I couldn't bear.

I could go home and be considered a success. I had made it across America! My mom would give me a big kiss, and Dad would say, "Welcome home, Son." My friends and I would get together, and I would tell some stories. Everything would be back to normal.

"Where are you going next?" I repeated in my head.

Then again, where was I headed in the first place? My idea in taking the bus was to trudge slowly across America to those places oft read about. I wanted to see the West Coast. I wanted to stick my pale white Pennsylvania butt in that water and say, "Yes! It is here! The Pacific ocean exists!" I didn't want people to tell me that the Rockies were beautiful; that Californians were weird; that Texas was a big state. I wanted to take my body and my mind there, and believe no one but myself and my experience. I wanted America to no longer be in maps and books and in the slides from some guy's trip to Florida, but a tangible piece of my own existence.

And now it seemed like I was willing to quit.

My mind wanted me to fly home, to take the safe, easy way out. Just like I had never questioned things in my life or challenged myself, I wanted to just quit because it would be the easiest thing to do.

But I also thought about all the things I had learned on this trip. I was asking questions of myself, for which I still did not have answers. I had met people on this trip who forced me to confront views I had taken for granted previously. I had been proven wrong about a number of things along the way. Did I really want to end this whole thing prematurely?

No, Quay. You may be a lot of things, but you're not a quitter. Even if it killed me, I decided that I was riding the bus back to Pennsylvania.

Once I had made the decision to keep going, I grew more excited about getting on the road again. It was nice to rest at my relatives' place, and I got the resentment of bus travel out of my system. Part of my excitement was going to be this ticket purchase. I was going to try the advice from the Floridian Jedi about purchasing a ticket across the country. I wanted to see if it was really going to work. My mind was spinning at the combinations I could make. The only thing I knew for sure was that I wanted to get to Greeley, Colorado.

Greeley isn't famous for any particular reason. I guess its most intriguing point is that it was named after Horace Greeley, the guy who said, "Go west young man." For me, though, it held a different interest. My best friend in college was named Kevin Greeley, and he was a long, lost descendant of Horace. At least that's what he told me. When I was looking over a map before I left Pennsylvania, I had spotted the name in Colorado. I promised Kevin, if I got that far, I'd go and take a picture. There was even more intrigue for me to get to Greeley, though.

Another friend of mine, Jim, had called me while in Seattle

and told me that he and his girlfriend were going cross-country. His father owned a Christmas tree farm in Bloomsburg, PA, the place where I went to college. Every December I would work for them, and we had grown quite close. He wanted to connect somewhere as they were traveling west and I was traveling east.

"Where do you want to meet, Hanna?" he asked me with his long, drawn out, Northern Pennsylvania, redneck accent.

"Greeley, Colorado."

Jim knew Kevin as well. Kevin worked his Decembers on the tree farm, too. He was the one who actually introduced us. Jim sounded a little startled at this rendezvous point.

"Where?"

"Greeley."

"Who would be dumb enough to name a city that? Whatever. What day are you gonna be there?"

"Probably Tuesday night. I'll find out when . . ."

"See you then."

And he hung up. Jim always liked to know the least amount possible so he could figure it out from there. Sometimes it was a really annoying. I remember one time when we were supposed to deliver 350 trees to one of our customers in New Jersey. He hadn't written the directions down, claiming he had them committed to memory, and we ended up driving around for five hours. Once there, we found out that we couldn't pull both the trailer and the truck next to the sales lot to unload. Instead we had to pull into an abandoned driveway 200 yards away. Then we carried each tree, one by one, and placed them on the sales lot.

The guy who had ordered the trees yelled, " What the #!@*& is going on here? That's going to take forever!"

But Jim just kept on carrying them, acting like the guy wasn't there at all. Jim was stubborn as a mule.

To be honest, I didn't really expect our meeting to take place for those very reasons. I figured by day two of their trip he would have thrown the map out the window claiming he had been on this highway in some other life. But I was excited nonetheless that there was a possibility.

I asked my aunt to drop me off at the station two hours before my departure time. I had called ahead about getting a one-way ticket to Pennsylvania that went through Denver, and they had said it would not be a problem. It just didn't seem like it should be that easy, so I wanted to make sure I got to the station in plenty of time to argue for as long as was necessary.

Norma and I pulled up in front of the big glass doors, and I grabbed my bag. She was looking at me through those glasses with the lenses that get darker when the sun shines on them.

"I think what you're doing is great, Quay."

"Thanks, Norni."

"I'm proud of you."

That meant a lot to me. I rarely heard those words. I also rarely met adults who were supportive of this trip across America. It was nice to get some validation.

I learned a lot in my short stay with my relatives here. They were nothing like the rest of my extended family. They went to the theater. They drank espresso. They ate Thai food. During my visit I was encouraged to try these things and it became a microcosm of my whole trip. It represented the chance of physically removing myself from the surroundings I had known forever and try something different. So I drank lattes. I ate some kind of fancy pizza called a pogacha. I went to a craft show and tried to appreciate the different types of art. I would never do this stuff at home. Partially, because I would be mocked the rest of my entire natural life. Also, though, I probably wouldn't do it just because I never had. Why bother?

While I was here, I began to see the danger in this type of thinking. That is where the learning ends and the rut begins. If I wasn't willing to give a gyro a try, how would I ever be able to reflect on any other point of view? If I stopped questioning, how would I ever know the truth? I had to abandon what I "knew" in order to find what I "believed." Realizing that is such a big step in life. Forget everything you know and start over.

I found that a lot of the time I came back to the things I had always known. I still take black coffee over a latte. Give me McDonald's over any fancy restaurant. I'd sooner take in a tractor pull than a craft show. And that's all right. Now my opinions are mine, though, no longer an opinion somebody fed to me.

I walked inside the bus station and was amazed at the scores of people. It was like a carnival was going on. As I walked in the front door, I looked past the rows of chairs to the ticket counter. The line was going off to the right and it bent around a corner so far, I couldn't see its end. I pulled myself up by my bootstraps and walked confidently to the end of the line, anxious to start this trip again.

I slowly made my way through the mob of people. There were kids running everywhere! Where could all these people be going on a Monday afternoon? I followed the long line back from the front desk, looking into the joyless, tired faces of the others who were waiting. I plopped my duffel bag down, and took up residence dead last in line.

The line moved as quickly as could be expected, and it was forty minutes until I had my chance. At first the attendant didn't want to give me the ticket.

"You have to take the northern route; Montana, Minnesota, Illinois . . ."

"No, no, no. I called and was told I could go down to Denver first and then take it from there."

There was frustration in the long string of passengers behind me, and I recognized that communal sigh heard when one moron is holding up the rest of the line. I looked around to see who the moron was, somewhat shocked to find out it was me.

The attendant finally called his supervisor who said, "Go ahead. In fact, from Denver would you rather go to Chicago or

Indianapolis?"

"Chicago, sir." I said with a big cheesy grin on my face as I looked at the young attendant who was pouting next to his supervisor.

He handed me the packet of tickets —10 of them in all— and I looked at the total mileage: 4,500 miles! 4,500 miles for $135! I was in my glory.

I had been in line so long and hee-hawing at the ticket desk that my bus was due to leave in fifteen minutes. I was happy that I had planned on getting to the station plenty early. As I sat, anticipating a fresh start on my adventure back to the east coast, I looked up and down the row of waiting riders. There was a strange characteristic I was seeing among these people. Four of them were cross-eyed. It wasn't any big deal, but I found it a little strange. I'd never seen so many cross-eyed people in one place in my life.

As we began to load, I decided to take a seat in the "action zone," I think mainly to show myself that I was ready to start the adventure afresh. I wanted to jump in strong. It was going to be a full bus. That was for sure. I watched as a lot of strange looking people boarded, but one couple especially caught my attention.

The lady was large and pink. She was a 275 pound woman stuffed into a matching pink sweatshirt/sweatpant combo. The sweatshirt had a logo on the front with a puffed up white kitten and a caption that read, "I'm not fat, I'm fluffy!" Fluffy had her curly red locks wadded underneath a hat with a picture of Goofy's head on the front, the excess hair flowing out both sides and hiding the arms of her glasses.

Her boyfriend was just the opposite. He was thin enough that I bet he would have fit between her butt-cheeks. He had long black hair and a goatee to match. His sleeveless black Harley T-shirt gave us all the opportunity to see how few weights he had actually lifted in his life. I think he believed he looked tough with it on, but he looked more like a fool since the temperature was about 1 degree outside. He was also one of the "special people" I had described earlier: cross-eyed. He was probably glad, though. It kept him from getting too good of a look at his girlfriend.

Fluffy had gotten the seat directly across the aisle from me, and was trying to get Tough Guy's attention by yelling, "I'm back here! I'm back here! D-a-a-an, I'm baaack heeeeere!" I felt like leaning over and saying, "Lady, even with two crossed eyes he ain't gonna miss you on this bus!"

After Dan had plopped down in the six inches of seat that was left next to her, she started yelling out the window to the group of eight people who were seeing the two of them off. These were non-opening windows, so Fluffy wasn't actually yelling out of it, but rather through it.

"Bye-bye! (kissing sounds) Aloha! Bidy-bye!"

The group outside was grinning and laughing and yelling back, but we couldn't hear them and I'm sure they couldn't hear her. It was like some kind of a comedy scene.

"Get Rachel! . . .No, Rachel! . . . Rachel!"

Rachel was outside the bus and didn't understand what Fluffy wanted, so she was forced to squeeze her massive butt-cheeks down the aisle again, even though we were leaving in about three minutes. I watched as she explained something to her gang, I assumed it was some kind of mental support group, and waddled back onto the bus, giggling and laughing, hardly able to contain herself. As she struggled back the aisle, she constantly looked through the windows, leaning over the seated passengers and shouting, "Wait!"

When she finally got back to her seat, she summoned Dan from his cross-eyed slumber and told him, "Watch! Now watch!"

She gave the go sign and the group delivered a great big Dating Game kiss. Fluffy purred victoriously.

I didn't do much talking going down the road. We were headed to Portland for our first bus switch and somehow I had gotten on an "express" bus. This meant that it didn't stop in all the little one horse towns in between the major cities. I didn't even know there was such a thing and I didn't know how I got on one, but I wasn't going to complain. I wasn't going to complain about the bus, anyway.

Fluffy, on the other hand, was annoying the crap out of me. She maintained a loud discussion with Dan the entire time, which was shared with the lot of us. The trip to Portland was four hours and I can't remember her being quiet for more than thirty seconds. She had to be driving Dan crazy. Forget Dan, she was driving me crazy.

Upon arrival in Portland, I immediately went to my exit for Salt Lake City, even though the bus wasn't leaving for another hour or so. I mentioned earlier that this was a smart move to assure a seat, but it was also a good place to meet potential riding partners. It was always worth the extra effort to try to find someone who seemed tolerable.

I was stunned again to notice the number of cross-eyeds waiting to board with me. It must have had something to do with the genes of all those California gold rushers, squinting all the time to see if that little rock was going to make or break them.

I sat in line and continued to watch the people, just hoping there would be one I would want to sit with. About that time a young guy walked by looking at his ticket, and then looking up at the exit number. He looked back down at his ticket, then back to the desk, then to the exit number.

"You need some help?" I offered, denying myself the personal laugh of calling him "Chief."

"Uh, yeah. Is this the exit for Salt Lake City?"

"It sure is." I said it with that air of confidence that comes from being a seasoned bus traveler.

He breathed a sigh of relief and dropped his bag next to mine. I waited for the verbal lynching that usually occurred when someone butted in line, but I guess no one was paying attention.

"Where you headed . . ." I offered.

"The name's Jeff. I'm going to Nashville."

"I'm Quay. . .with a Q. Nashville, huh? You a singer?"

"Sure am. Songwriter, too. Gotta go to where dreams come true, you know? How 'bout yourself?"

"Well, I'm headed to Denver at the moment. I've just been traveling about five weeks or so. I'm kind of on my return trip home."

"Wow, that's pretty cool. Like Kerouac, huh?"

"Well, not exactly. I just needed to get out and see some stuff. Know what I mean?"

"Yeah. I know what you mean. I quit college to pursue my music. I just couldn't deny what I wanted to do. I was only going to college for my parents anyway. Now everybody thinks I'm nuts! Sometimes I wonder myself. I mean, what if I fail? I'd have to go back to all those people in Eugene who told me I "lacked direction" and that I'd be back. I mean, what if I lose?"

I understood what he meant. I didn't really feel like I was in a position to give a lot of advice, but I had a thought on the topic.

"I relate my ambitions to a saying we used quite often when I harvested Christmas trees back in Pennsylvania: If you make your mornings, the afternoon takes care of itself. I consider youth to be our 'morning.' It is a time that we can take some chances, as there aren't a lot of others who are relying on us. If we go broke, it isn't really hurting anyone except ourselves.

The afternoon I consider everything after that. My thought when I left on this trip was that no matter what happens with the rest of my life, at least I can say I saw my own country. For now, that is what I consider 'making my morning.' I'm counting on the afternoon to take care of itself."

Jeff looked contemplative. He stared at me a second and then said, "You look like a redneck, but you talk like a philosopher."

"I guess I'm both," I replied.

We were suddenly interrupted by an announcement coming

over the loudspeaker.

"Attention Greyhound passengers.   Due to inclement weather, all buses out of Portland headed east have been canceled."

A communal groan passed through the crowd. I must admit that I was probably the loudest. I was trying to reestablish my bus moxie and this wasn't making it any easier.

"Anyone wishing to have their trip rerouted, please move towards. . ." and before the words were out, people were headed for the ticket window like we were on a sinking ship and it was the only life raft. People were falling over each other, jumping a three foot high wall in the center of the station, showing a complete disregard for one another.

I tried to figure out what everybody had to do that was so important. I chuckled and leaned over to Jeff.

"Look at all these people in a hurry to go nowhere."

He got out his notebook and started writing.

"What are you writing?" I asked nosily.

" 'Look at all these people in a hurry to go nowhere.' I like that. Maybe I'll use it in a song someday."

And since that Portland bus station, I have listened closely to every country song ever played to hear my words of wisdom so I can sue him for copyright infringement. No luck yet.

Since I was determined to know where my buses and connections would be, so a fiasco like the Vegas to Seattle trip would never happen again, I knew exactly what the departure time would be out of Salt Lake City for Denver. The fact was, it didn't matter what time we left Portland, there wasn't any way to catch our connection in Utah. Waiting the night in Portland would get us there at the same time as taking the rerouted trip that night. Why bother riding all those extra hours?

I shared this "insider tip" with Jeff, and though impressed with my quote earlier, he had his doubts about my bus logic.

"I think I'm going to get my ticket changed anyway," he told me as politely as possible.

"Well, suit yourself."

Another announcement came over the loudspeaker.

"For your convenience, Greyhound will provide rooms at a nearby hotel for only $30. Please show your ticket to the hotel manager to receive your discount."

I didn't want to do this either. It wasn't a bad deal, but the time was already 11:30 at night. I would have to be back at the station by 10:00 a.m. to be sure I was one of the first ones in line. I figured it was a waste of money to pay that much for a place to sleep. I also couldn't afford to miss the next bus if I wanted any chance at making the rendezvous with Jim.

"For those not interested in the hotel, you are welcome to stay at the station. There will be two security officers on duty until tomorrow morning."

Bingo. It was about time I slept on the bus station floor anyway.

With most people having left on other buses, and the rest headed to the hotel, there were only twenty of us staying at Greyhound Motel. I personally chose to sleep near the exit I was to be leaving from the next day. I had asked the lady at the ticket window which one it would be because I didn't want to miss the bus tomorrow, as I was already running fourteen hours behind schedule.

I laid on my back and propped my head on my duffel bag. The station was quiet and peaceful. As I looked around, I had to laugh at the strange assortment of characters I was sharing my sleeping quarters with that night. Myself and nineteen strangers napping in the Portland bus station.

By 5:00 a.m. I was awake for good. The night hadn't been too restful as one of my bunkmates kept standing up and shadow boxing in his sleep. He was yelling, "One, two! One, two!" as he threw left and right jabs. This guy, along with the cold, hard floor gave me little comfort or rest.

My reason for sleeping next to my exit was to be first in line to assure myself a spot on the bus, but it was still seven hours before we would be boarding. I didn't want to sit on the cold floor the whole time, so I decided to sacrifice a couple spots in line to afford myself the luxury of wandering around the station. My main goal was to get something to eat. Fortunately (or unfortunately, depending on how you want to look at it), the Greyhound eatery had fired up its grill at 6:30 and breakfast would soon be on the way.

As I sat down to relax in peace before the station became a bustling beehive, fear suddenly paralyzed me. Say it isn't so! Tell me it's a nightmare! Fluffy and Dan were walking directly towards my table! It was like slow motion. I had already started eating my food, so I couldn't pretend like I was taking it elsewhere. There were two seats at my table. All the forces of nature were directing these two towards me.

I looked down as I hurriedly shoved the potatoes in my mouth. If this interaction was to become a reality, I wanted to eat as quickly as possible and find some excuse to go elsewhere. I was hoping that by avoiding eye contact they would get the point that I wanted to be alone. Still looking down, I could feel the presence of a large shadow enveloping me. I figured it was either a solar eclipse or Fluffy. I dared not look up. Then I heard that whiny voice.

"Excuse me! Excuse me!"

I was trying to ignore her, pretending that she must have been talking to someone else, although her piercing voice could possibly lead *anybody* in the place to think she was talking to them.

Dan said, "Seems like he's deaf."

"Maybe you're right, honey. EXCUSE ME! CAN YOU HEAR ME? DO YOU NEED ME TO TALK LOUDER?"

It was obvious that I was not going to get out of this. The windows were shaking all around the station, and the louder she talked the more people were looking in our direction.

"What are ya'll looking at?! Have some respect for the handicapped!" she shouted at them.

"I can hear," I said, "I just wasn't sure that you were talking to me."

"Can me and my boyfriend sit with you? We're always looking to make new friends!"

What's a guy supposed to do, right? Have you ever known people like this? They just are completely unable to see that they annoy the crap out of others. People that are constantly complaining and tell you about it. People that don't realize that they aren't welcome. People who . . . wait a second here . . . I'm describing myself, so I better shut up.

"Sure," I said, as unconvincingly as I could.

The night had not been kind to Fluffy. Her curly hair was all flat on the side she'd been sleeping and her makeup had washed off, so she had zits coming through. She was still in her pink outfit, although I could see some stains in spots where little pieces of chocolate had fallen off her Three Musketeers.

Dan didn't look much worse for the wear. He was still jacketless and sleeveless. I was having difficulty forcing down my Greyhound breakfast as I stared at his armpit hair touching the table as he leaned forward. I assumed he did this because he couldn't see me through his crossed eyes. It was obvious neither had tasted a breath mint lately.

"Where ya' goin', friend?" Fluffy opened with.

I was hesitant to tell her. I know it's rude, but I just didn't want to start describing my trip to them. I knew they would want to hear all about it and I didn't feel like sharing.

"I'm going home." I responded as curtly as possible, while shoving the last of my food into my face.

"Awesome! Where's that?" They were both staring at me.

"Lancaster, PA."

"WHAT?! Do you know that's the whole way across the country?!"

"Yeah, I had some idea."

"How did ya' sleep?" she continued.

"Like crap."

"We know what you mean. We had to sleep on the hard floor, too."

"I think everyone did," I responded with a bit of sarcasm. I finished my food and was ready to end this conversation. I was just waiting for the right moment.

"Yeah, I know Sweetheart, but it was really tough for that lady over there," she said pointing across the station to a young woman holding an infant. "She and her baby were shivering. I got to talking with her, and found out she doesn't have much money. She is going to Indiana to stay with some family, but she has almost nothing with her. They just looked so sad and cold.

Me and Dan always come prepared, so we had two blankets with us; one for the floor, one to cover up with. We asked her if she wanted them. She was so thankful. We gave the stuff to her in case she ran into anymore snow cancellations along the way."

I sat in silence for a moment just staring straight ahead. Finally, after a brief moment, I said, "If you'll excuse me, I was just finishing up and I have a few things to do."

"That's fine, Sweetheart. Me and Dan saw you sitting over here and we just wanted to say we're glad you're traveling with us. You are a very polite young man. It's nice to have guys like you on a bus. Most people wouldn't let complete strangers sit with them at a table like this. We appreciate it."

I picked up my tray full of trash and started for the trash can. It was another one of those moments. I stepped back and saw how selfish I really was. I hadn't seen a woman with a baby in the station, and even if I had, I wouldn't have thought twice about them. I had been so wrapped up in my "survival of the fittest" mentality for the last few years that I didn't even consider people around me.

And here was Fluffy, a woman I had despised this whole leg of the trip, who was caring and considerate. Don't get me wrong, she was loud, obnoxious, annoying, and didn't stop aggravating me the rest of the trip, but it was through a person like her that I saw my own lack of concern for others. As a society we've become convinced that saints are quiet, kind, thin, people. Fluffy made me realize that they come in all shapes and sizes.

The station had opened its doors to the rest of the community, so people started rolling in. I was surprised that more riders hadn't joined me in line, especially Fluffy. I just sat in silence for a while as the station became more crowded and bustling.

The bus finally arrived and we trudged through the snow to ours. It was both a miserable and wonderful day to be on a bus. What I mean is that the weather outside was really slushy. It had snowed all night, but now it was raining, and the roads were covered with muck, which meant it was very slow travel. On the bright side, though, it was perfect for sleeping. I was in and out of sleep for a number of hours. The slow, dreary day began to turn into night, but the bus trudged on slowly. We were to be in Salt Lake City by morning, and my hope was that things would continue to go just as smoothly until we got there. It was getting later into the evening and I decided to lay back and get some sleep. I don't know how long I was asleep before I was awakened by these words:

"Excuse me, sir! Sir! Hey! Sir, excuse me!"

I was lying on my back in my favorite position, and when I opened my eyes, standing there was a large, older lady with a look of disgust.

"Sir, would you please get up!"

It finally came to me where I was, and I sat up abruptly and mumbled, "Sorry."

She sat down with a distinct thump to show her displeasure at my slow reactions. I knew I had been sleeping for a while, so I was curious as to how long. I looked at the sign above the station; Boise Greyhound. We were in Idaho.

As my eyes moved down from the sign and onto the

boarding passengers, a chill quickly ran down my spine. Through the fog and bus exhaust, I counted no less than six children getting on! I turned to the lady sitting next to me hoping she had turned into a unicorn or something, to tell me this was in my mind and not reality. Six children! I would rather 500,000 bees get on than six kids!

Luckily it was late at night and everyone went back to sleep, including the children. Actually, I think the whole bus got a good night's rest except for my riding partner, who informed me the next morning that I was laying my head on her and hitting her with my elbow.

"You were hitting me the whole time you were sleeping," she accused.

"I wasn't sleeping," I joked.

She didn't laugh.

The next morning we arrived in Salt Lake City forty-five minutes behind schedule. We didn't even go into the station, as the bus we were transferring to was already waiting for our arrival. They had held it for us. I hopped on and there sitting in the very first seat was my buddy Jeff from Portland! I told him I'd talk to him later, but he got off somewhere before me and I didn't see him again.

I moved towards the back, mainly because I knew the kids were going to be sitting near the front, and I wanted to be as far away from them as possible. I made my way back to the action zone, and suddenly an older, black guy grabbed my arm.

"Sit here, Bro."

I wasn't sure why he wanted me to sit with him, but I wasn't going to argue. He looked a bit menacing.

Directly across from me was a fat guy who was in full *dpm*. I'm not exactly sure who he was kidding, because it was going to be a full bus, no doubt about it. There was just no need for *dpm* if it was going to be full. It was better to choose a partner that you thought might be tolerable. In fact, that was probably what my partner had done. I don't know what made him think that some 23 year old hillbilly was tolerable, but either way he must of saw me as his best option. The Fat Guy across from us was soon going to wish he hadn't been in *dpm.*

All the seats were filled except the one next to Fat Guy and I thought maybe he had pulled it off. But something just didn't seem right about this bus. I couldn't put my finger on it, but it seemed like someone was missing.

And then I heard it.

That shrill laugh. That whiny, loud obnoxious voice. I looked forward to see the bus enveloped in pink. It was Fluffy. And she needed a seat.

She made her way up the aisle, as best she could, trying to squeeze her butt through and whacking people on the head with her bags. She was loudly saying, "Excuse me. Excuse me. Pardon my bag. Pardon me." She finally arrived at the seat across from us. She had positioned herself to face Fat Guy, which meant her butt was directly in my face. My riding partner was laughing out loud as I tried to stay out of the way, but each time she moved, one of her cheeks seemed to hit one of my cheeks, if you know what I mean. She stood there waiting for Fat Guy to move his stuff, but he didn't seem fazed by this at all. He had this cheesy smile the whole time, and when Fluffy asked to sit down, he just said, "no."

This was a problem. You had to let a person sit with you. *Dpm* was a suggestion that you'd rather be alone, and a nasty look usually turned people away. But to have the only seat left and say "no," well, it just wasn't done.

"Whadda ya' mean no?!?!"

"I said no." He wasn't being loud or arrogant. In fact, he continued to maintain a smile.

Fluffy stormed back up the aisle. As best she could, anyway. The woman bus driver came back and yelled,

"Who's refusing to give up their seat? Huh? I want to

know!"

I thought it was a dumb question since there was only one seat open, but I sure wasn't going to say anything. I thought this might get ugly.

"Was it you?" She asked Fat Guy forcefully. Again the obvious question directed at the obvious choice.

Fat Guy still sat there with that grin.

"I told her to go ahead and sit down. She thought I said 'no.'"

We all were trying to hold back laughter as he continued pleasantly smiling, while Fluffy was getting even angrier.

"Yes he did! Yes he did!" as she began to squeeze her butt in next to his. The sum of them both equaled about sixty inches of rear-end trying to be stuffed into a fifty inch space. I thought the handle to the aisle seat was going to bust off.

"Somebody skinny switch with me! Can somebody skinny switch with me?! Fluffy was bellowing throughout the bus. This was turning into a Saturday Night Live sketch.

Still with that grin on his face Fat Guy declared,

"I'm skinny!!"

We all busted out laughing.

Finally, some old guy offered to switch, which affected him less than his present riding partner. My partner leaned over and said, "Thanks for sitting with me. If she had sat here, I would have killed her."

My partner was a large, bearded black man named Don. His looks would have given the impression of being a pretty rough character, and though his voice was powerful, he really was mild mannered. I had to laugh when he complained that there were too many paper towels in the bathroom dispenser. I had never heard that complaint in my life.

"I don't understand. So what?" I asked him.

"That means people ain't washin' their hands! They ain't washin' their hands after goin' to the bathroom! That's sick, man.

Their parents didn't raise them right."

"Yeah," I said as emphatically as possible, placing my piss-stained hands underneath my butt.

The ride through the Rockies was incredible. The bus was traveling directly over the mountains, so travels were slow, but the scenery was unlike anything I had ever seen before. I didn't know there could be anything this beautiful in the world. Since it was winter, everything was snow covered, and this white background made it easy to see the antelope running around in search of food. Some people were complaining about the pace of the driving, but I blocked out the others and enjoyed the view from the window.

There was no place on earth I would have rather been.

Slow travels and fatigue caused tensions to rise and about nine hours into the journey it finally exploded.

"Would you knock it the #!@*& off!" resounded from the front of the bus.

We all craned our necks to see who it was. Swearing that loudly was a bus taboo, the punishment being that you forfeited your ticket. It was this middle aged black guy who was sitting near the six kids. He had two in front of him and two beside him. That's like being attacked from two fronts.

"How dare you yell at my children! Don't you ever use that language in front of them again!"

"Well, get control of them! This #!@*& chair is goin' up and back, up and back! My knees are black and blue! I'm sick of this #!@*& lady!"

Now the bus driver started getting into it.

"Sir, you do not use that language on my bus!"

"Ma'am, I'm sorry, but I'm just sick of it! I've been putting up with this sh . . . crap the whole way from Utah!"

"That is no excuse for your language! I want everybody off at the next stop!"

Everybody off? What in the world was she thinking? If I

was her, I would have diffused the situation by telling everyone to calm down and discussing it at the next stop. A lot of people had been complaining about her driving, though, and maybe she had had enough of it and was going to ditch us all there in the mountains.

We were in the heart of the Rocky Mountains. You could feel the elevation as you breathed. The bus pulled into what looked like a little ski chalet overlooking the mountains. It was a beautiful setting for an argument. All of us got off and it seemed like we were going to a beheading.

We stood in the warmth of the sunshine of the little parking lot. It was at the top of a steep mountain and overlooked the peaks and valleys of the Rockies. I was kind of glad the Swearer got in trouble, because it afforded me the opportunity to take in the breathtaking scenery. We weren't exactly sure what to expect, as none of us had ever seen the entire bus forced to unload. We all stood outside the bus, milling around and waiting for the Swearer's trial.

The driver was the last one to get off and she immediately began laying into him.

"Sir, I have every right to kick you off this bus! You do not swear on this, or any bus, anytime, anywhere!"

"Ma'am, I cracked. These kids have been a pain in the . . ."

The mother quickly interrupted to defend her parenting skills. "They're kids! They get tired! They get antsy!"

"Then you ought to teach 'em some patience!"

I was on the side of the black guy. If you're going to drag your kids on the bus, you'd better have decent control over them. We all paid good money and deserved to enjoy the ride as much as possible. Kids on the bus could be a nightmare. I don't necessarily blame the kids, though. It's a long time to sit. But consideration is learned at a young age, and these kids were lacking it.

The driver spoke. "Sir, I've got a good mind to tell you not to get back on!"

It sounded like his sentence was coming down without the driver even considering his defense. At this point, she hadn't even said anything to the mother.

He again pleaded his case.

"Look, maybe I should have used better language, but I was probably saying what a lot of people wanted to say."

The driver was unconvinced. "That's a poor excuse, and there is a good chance that your trip is going to end right here."

I'm not exactly sure what the driver was deliberating about, but she sure seemed wishy-washy. If she was going to kick him off, then she should just do it. Stop making threats.

Suddenly, Don spoke up, "If he ain't gettin' back on, neither am I!"

The crowd gasped and started to whisper.

I wasn't sure why Don was doing this. He didn't even know the guy. It wasn't like we were even sitting near him on the bus. Since they both were black, I thought maybe it was just to show support for a "brother."

I pulled Don aside.

"What are you doing?" I asked.

"Quay, let me tell you something about life. When you see something that is wrong, every now and then you have to stand up and make a statement, even if it costs you. This guy has a right to keep riding. I don't care what anybody thinks."

I thought about it. Don was right. It wasn't a black thing. It was a human thing. And I was a human.

Maybe Don's words got to me, or maybe I got caught up in the moment. Either way, I suddenly blurted out,

"If they don't get back on, then I don't either!"

I knew this wasn't prudent. If we got stuck at this ski chalet, I knew I probably didn't have enough money for a room. And if I didn't have money for a room, how exactly was I going to get out of here? And, Don and the Swearer: I didn't really know these guys. Would they help take care of me?

But I felt it was something I had to do. I had learned a lot on this trip. Maybe I was going to stop seeing things in black and white. Maybe I was going to start standing up for what I know is right instead of backing down all the time because it is "inconvenient." No matter what motivated me that day, it was a turning point in my life.

There was a sudden clamoring of voices and the supporters of the woman stood with her, and our supporters congregated behind us. Lost in all this were the kids who were throwing snowballs at each other.

Before the mutiny went any further, the driver pronounced,

"All right! All right! Sir, a simple apology to the lady and the promise to watch your language is what I need from you."

"I'm sorry."

"Ma'am, I need you to watch your children a little closer to keep them under control."

"I will."

The driver looked about at the silent crowd as if waiting to hear any more complaints or social uprisings, but nothing being spoken she hollered, "Let's get going!"

While the others started getting back on the bus, I stood off by myself to contemplate the scenery. Here I stood high above America at the great Continental Divide, a different and better man. These mountains represented the mountains I had climbed in my own life and on this trip. I was headed east again, having seen the west and knowing it truly exists. I had confronted myself and realized that though I knew my own existence, there was much more I could do with it. The progression of a trip, and the progression of my character. Yeah, I was going home. But I was never going to be the same again.

8

I hooked up with Jim in Colorado, spending six days traveling to the surrounding states. He dropped me off in Greeley and my bus adventure was to begin again. My last stop before home was South Bend, Indiana to see my old buddy, John. He graduated from Notre Dame and still lived in the area. He and I were close in high school, but I hadn't seen him since graduation. I thought this would be a great time to reconnect.

I left Greeley early in the morning and arrived in Denver around 11:00 a.m. I directly went to my departure exit. The sun was shining brightly through the huge plate glass windows. As I sat Indian style on the floor, basking in the warmth of the sun, I heard one guy talking above everyone else. I looked and saw a neatly dressed man around fifty years old. He was spewing from the mouth about any topic that came up and every response was loud. There were people sitting, listening, laughing, and agreeing with him each time he made his "point." I couldn't understand what they were getting from this guy. He wasn't clever and he wasn't intelligent.

"NBA Basketball?! Let me tell you the problem with those overpaid SOBs . . . "

"David Karesh?! He's that hopped up freak who thinks he's Jesus. You know what they oughta' do with that guy?! Why, they oughta . . . "

"Madonna?! That little sleazy, slutty porno star?! If I had any say in it, she'd . . . "

I can't stand people like this. People so insecure in their arguments that they figure the louder they talk, the more validity it gives to their statements. The Loud Mouth reminded me of a guy on my soccer team in college. The soccer guy got to be so despised, beating him up at freshman initiation became a tradition. They still do at the alumni events.

When the bus arrived, I made sure Loud Mouth got on before me, because there was no way I was sitting with him, let alone near him. Luckily he sat in the "sleeper zone," and I walked past him, straight to the back. Someone was in my favorite number 8, so I chose 9 instead.

I wasn't paying much attention to the boarding passengers. I was engrossed in trying to catch up on my journal. Suddenly I felt the bus tip forward. I didn't look up from my journal, but a second later I felt the bus sink again. For a moment I thought maybe both front tires had blown. Now I was curious.

I peered around the bodies in the aisle and almost screamed in fright. There was a huge mound of flesh and hair making its way back the aisle. Behind it was another. And another. And then some smaller ones. I quickly glanced outside the bus to see if they were filming a science fiction movie or something. What was going on?

When it got nearer, I realized that it was a man. He was about 6'4", 350 pounds., with long matted hair, and a sneer that would scare Steve Austin into submission. His contorted face protruded through a beard that contained more hair than all the bodies of the other passengers combined. He suffered from "dunlap" disease. His belly "dun-lapped" over his belt.

The belt was holding up a pair of plain pocket jeans, worn white in many spots, and coming up short of hiding his once white socks. He wore a flannel shirt, of which the buttons were being sorely tested in holding back his massive chest and gut. For warmth, his outer shell was a ragged hooded sweatshirt, with one of those down vests last seen in the early eighties.

The person behind him was his wife. She, too, was suffering from "dunlap" disease, but she was shorter, more rotund as opposed to humongous. I'd bet she was still five-nine though. She had long greasy hair and was missing two front teeth. Being repulsed, I couldn't stare long enough to get a good look, but I'm pretty sure she also had a beard. She was dressed like her husband, except for a baseball hat.

Following close behind were their four precious offspring, the oldest sixteen and the youngest around six, all of whom were very large, very loud, and very dirty in their own right. The Von Trapps they were not.

They came on like a hurricane, overtaking everything in their path with a flurry of cussing, hollering, and complaining. They were headed straight to the back. I noticed that the others around me had a similar look of disbelief on their faces, and I waited for someone to snap a picture to send to National Geographic with proof of a bigfoot family residing somewhere in Colorado.

I was hanging my head in disappointment at what I thought might transpire on this trip when I heard,

"Hey! Hey you! Can I sit here?"

I looked up to see a guy staring at me through a pair of glasses so thick and magnified, it made his eyes look like they made up half his face. He was short, but stacked with muscles which he showed off by wearing a tank top even though the temperature was about eight. He almost acted retarded.

I answered as generously as possible. "Uh, no . . . I mean, yeah . . . go ahead."

The adventure to Chicago had begun.

I decided to see what my partner had to say.

"So where you headed?"

"Aw, a #!@*& ways up," was his reply.

"Oh yeah? Whereabouts?"

"You ain't never #!@*& heard of it."

"I . . . see."

I went on to try several more times, only to be met with a combination of nonsense and cuss words. Before long I just sat quietly and began to feign sleep.

While I was pretending to catch some shut eye, the back few seats, inhabited by the entire cast from *Deliverance* got lively.

Actually, it sounded like a bad R-rated movie. The father would yell to the kids, "Shut the #!@*& up!" and then the kids would shout it at each other. At one point the sixteen year old daughter said to her little brother,

"Knock it off you little #!@*&."

Pa Ingalls was furious.

"You watch your #!@*& language, young lady!"

So pathetic, yet so comical. There wasn't a word of peace spoken among them. For some reason, my riding partner felt he had to get into the act.

"I wouldn't let my kids talk to me that way!"

"Mind your own #!@*& business!"

Since I could no longer pretend I was sleeping, because one would have to have been dead or unconscious to do so, I watched and waited to see what was going to happen next. My partner — the Harasser— would say something to the Hillbilly Dad and then turn to me for acknowledgement. I didn't want to agree, for fear of being sat upon by one of the big butts, but I didn't want to disagree for fear of my partner losing his own senses. So, I basically did a lot of shoulder shrugging, trying to remain as neutral as possible.

Somehow the situation defused itself, mainly because the Hillbillies went back to fighting amongst themselves and my partner decided to back out.

The bus started to quiet down. I had been faking sleep for a while, but I was feeling restful. The mutants had stopped arguing for the time being and most people were sitting and listening to the gentle hum of the Greyhound. It was relaxing after the incessant fighting.

And then it happened.

While we sat in our peaceful state, a giant but muffled splash was heard from the bathroom. Eyes wandered from seat to seat as we were hoping and praying it wasn't true. There was a bit of misery in the eyes of all the riders when that door finally opened and the youngest hillbilly stuck his dirty, crying face out and screamed, "Mommy, I just threw up!"

In her gentle motherly way, she answered,

"Well, get the #!@*& out of there before you get it all over yourself!"

She yanked him by the arm and pushed him into his seat.

The crowd sat in amazement as Mother Hillbilly did nothing more than fade back into slumber, without any notion of cleaning up her son's contribution to the bathroom. In the quietness of shock, the only voice heard was the sixteen year old cussing out her brother, because now she couldn't use the facilities.

There was nothing we could do. No one wanted to say anything out of fear. At least that was my excuse. I was scared of these people.

My riding partner didn't have the same sense as us, or else he was brave beyond measure. Whatever the reason, he spoke up for all of us.

"Clean up that #!@*& mess in there!"

"Mind you own #!@*& business you #!@*&!"

"It is my business! Where the #!@*& are we suppost' to piss?! There's puke everywhere!"

"Just shut the #!@*& up!" chimed in the daughter.

"You keep your #!@*& mouth shut!" the father lovingly responded to his daughter. Then he looked back at my riding partner and with a demonic scowl and in a voice straight from the pit of hell, he said,

"If you want the #!@*& puke cleaned up, you clean it up. That's that!"

And, indeed, that was that. I think the Harasser realized if a fight broke out it was 1000 pounds of redneck versus him.

I was among a group of eight or so that approached the bus driver at our next stop.

"Sir, a young man threw up in the bathroom!" said the one lady.

"What do you want me to do about it?"

His reply was smug, coarse, and not at all what I expected.

"Well, could you clean it up, or have somebody clean it up?"

"Look lady, my shift is up in two hours and then it's the next driver's problem. I sure ain't doin' it. So, it's either up to the mother or the next driver."

We stood perplexed at his reply. There was nothing for us to do, but board ever so slowly knowing what lay ahead for us. Eventually that smell was bound to leave the bathroom, and when it did, who knows what kind of puke chain reaction would result.

A few hours later we stopped for dinner at McDonald's. It was nice to get off the bus and away from the lunatics. We were told to get our food to go because we had lost time somewhere. Off and right back on again. As I stood there waiting in line, a little bit of depression set in. Was the rest of this trip going to be this lousy? How bad was the vomit smell going to get? Would they ever stop fighting? I was tired of everything about this journey. It was close to being as miserable as the trip to Seattle. This time, though, I didn't have a guy like Scott to share it with. I knew I wouldn't be switching buses for at least twelve hours, so I had to do something to turn the tide. That might mean fighting the giant, but I had to do something.

I was one of the first ones to get my food, so I went outside to get away from people for a little bit. I tried to gut it out sitting in the wind, but my secret sauce was blowing all over me and it had gotten pretty cold. I took the lonely walk to the bus and looked it over. I didn't want to get back on, but there was no use avoiding the unavoidable.

I sauntered back to my seat and let out a big sigh. I slowly pulled out my french fries when I noticed a guy near the front of whom I was truly envious. His riding partner had gotten off an hour ago, and he was enjoying his McNuggets far from the smell of the bathroom, far from the noise of the Hatfields and McCoys, right in the heart of the "sleeper zone."

As I looked longingly at his favorable position, the bus taboo of switching seats crossed my mind again. What would it matter? This time was a little different though. Like I had mentioned earlier, to have an extra seat to yourself on a bus this crowded was like gold. I wasn't a new rider. I had a seat. That was the first taboo, the same as the bus from Dallas to Las Vegas.

But to abandon my riding partner during the "war" was extremely rude. It suggested that I didn't care for his company (even though it wasn't a suggestion. I didn't.). To be honest, if he weren't so muscular and insane, I probably wouldn't have cared what he thought. I just didn't want him to freak out and beat me silly.

I deliberated a couple of minutes, finally deciding that I would rather take the beating than survive another minute in the back with those morons. I was rebel enough to break the unwritten laws.

I approached the man and put on a pathetic face. He looked up from his burger, but didn't say anything.

"Sir, uh, I was wondering . . . You have this extra seat and I'm . . . uh . . . you see . . . "

Spill your guts, Quay, you sissy!

"Some kid threw up in the bathroom, and it really smells back there. Plus, all the people are fighting and arguing, including my riding partner. I'm just really tired of it. I know you have your own seat here, but I was wondering if you'd be willing to let me move up here. I'd really appreciate it."

He looked at me like I was strange to make such a big production and simply said, "Go ahead."

I went back, scooped up my gear and moved into my new location. Not wanting to annoy the new guy, I kept my mouth shut and ate my Big Mac in peace. My eyes were on my sandwich for a second, when I looked up and saw a pretty, young blond-haired girl getting on the bus. I couldn't believe that I hadn't noticed her before.

I was quickly swallowing and wiping the slop off my face so I could smile at her when she went by, but instead she nestled up in the aisle seat directly across from me! Oh what a change in scenery! From the demons to an angel! What a smart move! I held off talking to her right away, since I was the new guy and I wasn't sure if I was going to have to survive another period of being a pariah before gaining acceptance.

My last order of business was to explain to my old riding partner that it was no fault of his that I had wanted to move. (What he didn't know wouldn't kill him.) He noticed I had moved immediately upon boarding.

"Hey, what the #!@*& are you doing?"

This made me a little nervous, as I had some hopes that he would just pass on by, forgetting that I was sitting with him in the first place. No such luck though.

"Uh . . . I just couldn't stand it back there with that smell and everything, you know? I have a really weak stomach. Plus that family. They're just so . . . you know . . . loud."

"Yeah. They're #!@*& sick people is what they are!"

Well, he was very understanding which either meant I had used the right words or he didn't care. I figured it was the latter, but I was still free! He smiled and walked back into the swamp once known as the "action zone."

I sat back and began to enjoy my dinner, laughing as the hillbillies came on with their numerous garbage bags of hamburgers. I watched as a young employee was sent out with a ladder, and forced to climb up in the blustery weather to change the sign. "Sold out."

About a half hour into the ride I hadn't said anything to anybody. I wanted to let my new riding partner make the move if he had anything to say, and I was waiting for just the right time to take on my blond-haired beauty. I don't think people were avoiding me because of the "seat switcher" stigma, as much as the fact that it was the "sleeper zone" and there was just a lot less discussion in this area.

I caught her looking in my direction and I made my move.
"Hi."

Man, am I smooth.

"Hi," she replied in her sweet little voice.

I've always been a sucker for blond hair, and hers was beautiful. I was also attracted to her by what she was wearing. It was a full sweatsuit. I like the look of fleece. I was hoping she was an athlete.

"Where ya' headed?"

"Hastings, Nebraska."

"Wow! I've never met anyone going to Nebraska."

Nice line, Idiot.

"Yeah. I'm transferring from my community college, to be with my twin sister in Hastings. She plays soccer there and she wanted me to come up and play too."

I was right! She was an athlete! Plus there were two of them! This was getting good. I imagined her offering to put me up a couple nights in Hastings and us falling in love and me moving to Nebraska. Nebraska? I wasn't sure if it was a dream or a nightmare.

"I played soccer in college, too. Bloomsburg University of Pennsylvania."

"Never heard of it."

"Yeah. It's a small school, but our soccer team was pretty good. I was captain my senior year."

I wasn't being completely honest now. It was a small school. I was captain. But we pretty much sucked every year.

By the time I had finished explaining each and every goal I scored, she had dug out her walkman and was rewinding, oblivious to anything coming out of my mouth. I found in bus travel that the walkman was a polite way of saying, "I've had enough of you now." Apparently she wasn't impressed with my athletic prowess. I didn't take it too hard. I wasn't that attracted to her anyway.

Okay, I'm not being completely honest here . . .

We arrived in Lincoln, NE around 9:30 p.m.. Blondie had gotten off a while back, and I hadn't talked to anyone else. I spent most of the time writing in my journal until it got dark. We had a short break here, so I got off to stretch. Greyhound employees were rushing past me with mops, buckets, and that kitty litter stuff.

"I can't believe the driver didn't clean that up hours ago!" I heard one say.

"It's such @#$%!" exclaimed another.

I felt bad for these guys. Six-hour vomit spread throughout the bathroom. They didn't even have the chance to face the driver who had left it, because his shift had ended two hours ago and the present driver had figured that if we'd made it four hours, we could handle another two. The drivers were passing the buck to the low men on the totem pole. Of course, I didn't offer to help, nor did I want anything to do with it, so maybe I should shut my big mouth.

Regardless of who had to do it, I was happy that the puke was cleaned up, but we received some potentially bad news while in Lincoln. There was some bad flooding and we were going to have to take an alternative route to Omaha. Once there, it was a possibility that no more buses would be running the rest of the night, in which case we would be spending the evening in the Omaha bus station. Images flashed through my mind of being curled up on the floor with a half ton of Hillbillies, nestled into the bosom of Momma Hillbilly. And then Hillbilly Harasser coming over to save me, only then to claim that we were going steady.

I began to shudder.

We moved on into the night, and the bus stayed relatively peaceful the whole time. I even got a little sleep before we arrived in Omaha around 1:00 a.m..

The scene there was a zoo, so my bus fit right in. Because of the flooding delays, there were many buses running behind. People were frenzied, afraid that they weren't getting anywhere. They had to go somewhere. They wanted to make progress.

It made me laugh. If you put these people on a bus, even in the wrong direction, they would consider it progress, because they were moving. "Oh, I'm not in the station so I must be getting somewhere." Although I laughed at them and their opinions on progress, I also realized that it wasn't too long ago that my own view of "progress" was much the same as theirs.

As I sat pondering my ideas, I noticed my riding partner sitting alone drinking a Dr. Pepper. I still hadn't said anything to him, appreciative of his kindness and respecting his peace, but I began to wonder if maybe the reason he let me sit there was because he wanted to talk with somebody and I had been a big disappointment to him. This section of my trip was winding down and I wanted to speak with him at least a little bit.

I bought my own soda and sat down next to him.

"This place is wild, huh?"

"Sure is. 'Specially with them fat rednecks runnin' round."

I busted out laughing and offered my hand.

"The name is Quay. . .with a Q. I'm headed to Pennsylvania."

"I'm Tom. I'm goin' back to Iowa."

"Is Iowa your home?"

"Sure is. I work construction there, but every winter I gotta go down south and get work. There ain't nothin' to do in construction in winter."

"I know what you mean. I'm in landscaping and construction. My boss kept me busy until January."

"Then what'd you do?"

"Well, I started this trip. I've been traveling around America for the last seven weeks."

"No kidding?! Good for you, man. I always wanted to do that."

They had called for us to get back on the bus, and to the

enjoyment of all, the half ton family was going no farther. I still sat with Tom though, and we talked shop for an hour or so before he got off in Des Moines.

I stood up to let him out. He stuck out his hand and said, "Hang in there. See the world, man. Do it now."

"Thanks."

It was now time for me to sleep. I hadn't rested at all since Idaho and I was having trouble remembering if it had been today or the day before. Whatever the case, it had been a long time. I was out like a light and didn't wake up again until 7:00 a.m. when we stopped for breakfast.

I was groggy as I stumbled into the restaurant, unaware of where we were in the United States. I ordered biscuits and gravy, mainly because it was the first thing on the menu, and started drinking coffee to get my juices flowing. I had started to dig into what appeared to be my meal when my eyes were opened as I heard a familiar voice.

"Liberals?! Those commies! You know what we oughta do with them? We oughta . . . "

It was Loud Mouth! I hadn't heard from him since Denver! I was going to have enough trouble forcing down this breakfast without listening to him. Apparently he had made some new friends on the bus, one of them telling him she majored in French while in college.

"French? I had a 93 in French in high school!"

He was bragging about a high school grade. I wanted to wheel around and say, "Who gives a rat's rear-end, buddy? Nobody cares. Nobody cares what you got in high school. You're fifty years old, for crying out loud! Just shut your big fat mouth!"

"Yeah, I was in Vietnam. I was like Rambo! No fear!"

That was enough. I couldn't digest this, nor my breakfast, so I got up and went outside. He won.

I stood outside shuffling my feet and it was soon time to leave. I had to laugh as three guys came running up and pounded on the door. They were inside finishing their pancakes when the driver said the bus was leaving. One thing I noticed about the drivers, when they said the bus was leaving, it was leaving. "We're pulling out of here at 8:30." And we did. There were no headcounts or double checking. You were either on it or you weren't.

We crossed into the Chicago city limits four hours later. I had decided to head straight to South Bend, but I had a two hour layover in Chicago. I had only left a message at my friend John's place where I was hoping to stay, and that was back in Seattle. I hadn't seen John in two years, so I'm sure he was probably pretty surprised to hear me on his answering machine. I had gotten paranoid, though. I didn't tell him what day, what time, what month, anything. He was a businessman. What if he was away on business? I started thinking that I should have planned a little better.

I called my mom because I wanted her to call John and give him all my pertinent information. You have to understand, this was in a time before cellphones. I was doing all the calling on an old-school payphone in the bus station. Instead of calling him, though, *my* mom called *his* mom, and had her call John. I called my mom back, and she gave me John's girlfriend's number in Iowa, telling me that John's mom wanted me to call her. I thought that was kind of dumb, since I had never spoken to her in my life. I had never even seen a picture of her. In fact, I wasn't even that good of friends with John, and now I was calling his girlfriend in Iowa who would have no idea who I am?

At one point, I started laughing imagining him walking into his apartment to find fifteen messages on his machine, all announcing my arrival.

The bus got to Chicago around 4:00 p.m. and we began boarding. I was happy to see that there were only fifteen of us on it. I was exhausted from all my dialing and fell right to sleep.

When I woke up, it was completely dark out, and another shot of paranoia ran through me. What happened if I had slept through my stop? No. Surely I would have heard the announcement, right? I couldn't be sure. It was dark. Was it 5:30 p.m. or was it midnight? I wasn't the watch wearing type, and at the moment, I wished that I was.

I sat glued to the window trying to read every road sign that flew by the window.

Nothing. Wait, here comes one! Ahh, shoot, I missed it.

Finally it appeared: South Bend 20 miles.

We arrived around 9:00 p.m. and I called John. I hadn't seen him in two years and when he walked into the station and saw me with my long hair, beard, and smelling of bus station, vomit, cigarettes and body oder, he probably figured that was the last time I had showered as well.

"I got your message," was the first thing he said.

9

John and I had little in common other than the past. We spent most of our time rehashing bits from our younger days and spoke almost nothing of the present. I always thought this would come later in life. Wasn't talking about the good old days what old people do? I guess people in relationships always try to find some common ground, even if all they have is the past. There's nothing wrong with that, but I knew it was time to move on.

Although I was leaving, my plans had changed. During my stay in South Bend, the blizzard of '93 hit the East coast. Mom had called and the city of Lancaster was completely shut down. I had planned on being home in the next two days, but now that didn't seem possible. I had to get on the road, though. I couldn't handle one more story about what we had for lunch our junior year of high school.

Since I had money left, I called Jon in Alabama again. I thought the weather there might not be as cold. Receiving word that the temperature was going to be in the seventies for the next few days, I decided to head south again before returning home. John drove me to the station (along the way we talked about our career stats in junior high soccer) and I made my way towards the gate.

There was still a half hour before departure time. Greyhound gave us the option of sitting on the bus or sitting in the station. I wanted to secure a good seat, so I opted for the bus. I watched out the window as the snow began to fall and passengers slowly began arriving. A pretty young girl wandered onto the bus and sat across from me. I wondered if the girls were actually getting more attractive, or if I had been riding so long that most anyone was turning me on.

"Hi," I said deciding to break out my best line right away.

"Hi," she responded.

"Sure is cold, huh?"

This was going well.

"Yep," and with that she pulled out her headphones.

I'm quite impressive, aren't I?

I looked back out the window and witnessed a very unattractive girl giving an unattractive smooch to an unattractive guy. Satisfied my visual judgment was still intact, I watched as she boarded and began heading towards me. As she got closer, I realized she was more homely than I first thought. She had spiked black hair on top of her eggplant shaped head, and in the middle of her face sat a pair of black, horn-rimmed glasses. She didn't have a jacket, but a long-sleeved sweater that came short of her pants, exposing the extra flab caused by her too-tight black jeans.

She sat behind me.

"Sure is cold." she offered.

"Uh, yeah," I said, wishing I had the guts to tell her she was giving us both chills with her too-short sweater.

"My name is Jen, where are you headed?"

"Quay, with a Q. I'm going to Tuscaloosa."

"Oh, yeah? I'm headed to Atlanta, Clay. I'm a student at Georgia Tech."

I wasn't in the mood to talk. I still had my mind on the pretty girl who hadn't even given me a shot. Unfortunately, Jen wasn't going to give me an opportunity to get away.

"Yeah, I'm a student at Georgia Tech. We just finished spring break. I came back to South Bend to spend time with my fiancée," she said, throwing that out in case I was getting any funny ideas.

"Wow, Georgia Tech. Is that a big school?"

"It's not big, but very elite. They only accept three percent of the applicants. They took me no problem though."

"Oh yeah?" I didn't like where this was going.

"I'm doing very well there. I've been on the dean's list every semester I've attended. I guess that's the reason I got a full scholarship. Of course, college isn't all that difficult if you just apply yourself . . . "

As she talked, I pulled out my headphones.

I listened to music the rest of the ride to Indianapolis. Luckily, Jen boasted of her intellectual prowess to another sap, so I didn't feel too bad about blowing her off.

Seat pickings were sparse when I boarded my next bus and I chose a spot with an older, black lady near the back. As I shuffled my things to get them in order, I caught her staring and smiling at me.

"Howdy, ma'am. You don't mind if I sit here, do you?"

"Only if you stop callin' me ma'am. I ain't that old," she said laughing and grabbing my arm.

"It's a deal." I acknowledged. "Where are you goin'?"

"Nashville. How 'bout yourself?"

"Tuscaloosa. I'm from Pennsylvania, but I'm trying to run away from the snow."

She burst out laughing, and from that point laughed at almost everything I said. It was nice to get such hearty guffaws as I told stories from the road, but I couldn't tell if she genuinely found me funny or if it had something to do with the whiskey I smelled on her breath. Either way, I didn't mind. I entertained her for an hour, but she eventually faded off to sleep. Alcohol and I have the same effect on people, too much of either will knock you out.

We rode into the night. I laid my head against the window, staring out at the combination of darkness, roadsigns, and headlights. I was headed back to Tuscaloosa and it seemed like a lifetime since first traveling there. I thought about this trip around the country which was coming to an end. I also thought about who I was at the beginning of the journey and who I was now. They were not the same two people.

I had always tried to shelter myself from those I hated. Fortunately, there was no getting around these people as a bus rider. Even more amazing, not only do you sit and talk with those you hate, you end up not hating them any longer. It is easy to hurl racial slurs and complain about people among your own kind. It is completely different when you sit and look at people you label face-to-face, realizing they are brothers, sisters, sons, daughters, friends, and neighbors - the same as you. The gap between black and white had always seemed huge to me. Sitting and interacting made me realize that we are much more similar than dissimilar. The things that separate us are superficial compared to that which links us together as humans. I'm not sure where I would have learned this had I never set foot on the bus.

I had always lived in fear. The problem with fear is that it typically digresses into hatred. That's what happened to me. I hated people. I didn't trust anyone who wasn't like me. I didn't talk to anyone who wasn't like me. I always felt other groups thought they were better than me, so I decided I would hate them. A lot of hatred is actually rooted in the fear of one another.

But I wasn't afraid anymore, and subsequently, I didn't hate anymore either. As a society, we focus our attention on organized hate groups. We think they are the root of hatred in the America, but they're not. They are a reflection of how far hatred can take you, but they are not the primary problem. It is our personal hatred of one another that perpetuates the issue.

As erudite as I may sound, I'm not. I learned all this traveling around the country - physically, mentally, and spiritually challenging all I believed to see America.

We rolled into some little city around 6:30 a.m. I had a headache and the weather was overcast. Through the fog I saw a lone passenger waiting to be picked up, and I watched as he slowly made his way to the door of the bus. It was a young, black man dressed in an Army uniform, carrying a duffel bag as big as himself. He struggled to get it on the bus, and since I had the only empty seat, he was forced to yank it down the aisle, disrupting the sleeping passengers as he did so.

"O.K. if I sit here?" he asked.

"Go ahead," I replied, resisting the urge to say, "Well, where else are you going to sit?"

We sat in silence a few minutes and he finally asked me,

"Where ya' headed?"

"Tuscaloosa. Where are you going?"

"South Alabama. To be with my wife. I've been over in Germany for the last six months and she's just been diagnosed with cancer." He paused a moment, "I just gotta' get home."

Though I had been traveling for weeks, I still found it very difficult to answer when a complete stranger shared something so intimate.

"Is she all right?"

"I really don't know. It all happened so fast. I just don't #!@*& know. I'm worried about my kids, though. One's three and the other thirteen months. It's got to be tough on them, especially since they're staying with my in-laws."

"Yeah. It can be hard for kids to be away from home," I said as if I had any understanding of children."

"It's not even that. My in-laws are #!@*&holes."

I looked at him a second, wondering if I should laugh. A big smile crossed his face and I smiled back, recognizing he was trying to break the tension.

"Why are you going to Tuscaloosa?" he asked.

"Well, I'm going there to visit a friend. I've been traveling around America for the last eight weeks and my trip is almost complete."

As I spoke those words, I was startled. It was the first time I comprehended that I had really done it. It wasn't just conversational chatter about what I was going to "do with my life."

I had taken the trip of which I had always dreamed.

"That's awesome, man. Good for you. I wish I had done something like that. But, you know, you get to thinking that marriage and family is what you really want. And then -BAM!- you're there. No way to get out after that. Don't get me wrong. I love my wife. I love my kids. I really, really, do. But, you know how things go. . ."

Yeah. I knew. That's why I was sitting on that bus.

"The name's Kevin."

"Mine's Quay. Nice to meet you."

We arrived in Birmingham a few hours later, and both Kevin and I had layovers. We bought breakfast at the station and sat down in the middle of the lounge area. The place was empty and relatively quiet. As we were enjoying our food, he asked me through a mouthful of hash browns,

"What are race relations like in Pennsylvania?"

It caught me off guard. Despite the changes I had made during this trip, I wasn't sure how to answer. Should I tell him about my past? Should I tell him that I was a racist before I left on this trip? Should I tell him I changed? What if he didn't believe me? I had *never* talked about racism with a black man.

"Well, they're not great. We don't have much interaction between blacks, whites, and other groups."

"Yeah. That's always a problem. Probably the main problem. So how did you avoid becoming prejudiced?"

I sat like a statue, staring forward trying to think exactly how I was going to answer the question. Kevin was chomping away at his sandwich while I was ready to crap my pants. He hadn't minced words about his wife's cancer, and now he was being uncomfortably straightforward about racism. Could I be honest?

"I don't know. You just figure people are people, I guess. A person's skin color can't determine what kind of a man he is, right? How could you automatically assume anything about anybody?

You know?"

The words came out slowly, and quietly. Kevin had been so honest and forthright from the beginning, and here I was lying right to his face. I had my head lowered and I probably seemed to be speaking more to the ground than to him. I felt ashamed.

"Well said, my friend. It's refreshing to meet someone from the country with a perspective like yours. City folk like me are told country boys like you are racist. To be honest, I wasn't sure what to think when I saw that the only seat left was the one next to you. I thought you might be a racist. I'll admit it went through my mind. I try not to stereotype people, but sometimes I do it anyway. Even so, I try and give everyone a chance and always hope they'll do the same for me. Thanks for proving my stereotypes wrong."

I sat in embarrassment at his honesty. I wanted to tell him about who I was at the beginning of this trip, but I couldn't. I wanted to purge myself of all the awful things I used to say about people, but I just kept it inside. I saw myself as the hate filled racist I was, and I wanted to leave it behind. At some point we should face those that we mock and criticize and hate, and then sit down and try to explain why we believe what we do. It forces you to see your belief for what it really is.

I didn't want to sit in silence, so I asked, "How do we help other people see the benefit in giving each other a chance?"

"Listen, Friend. We can do all the organizing we want. Hold demonstrations, make billboards, sign petitions. The bottom line, though? The real truth? It won't matter. If people don't judge others by color, then it will be by height. If not height, it will be hair color. No matter what we think, there will always be prejudice of some sort. But there is something we can do that will make a difference. We can raise our kids to be respectful and understanding. We can teach them to critique people based on their actions, not their skin color. We can teach them to listen to other cultures, and be willing to respect differences, even if we don't agree with them. That's what we can do. That's what guys like you and

I have to do."

I just sat quietly and soaked it all in. Here I was in Birmingham, Alabama, one of the most storied cities in the South. A place where segregation did not die easily. A place with a racist history the same as me. But it had changed. And so had I.

I heard them call my bus. I began to get myself together, too overcome with emotion to really say any more. I tend to talk a lot. I learned so much more in this moment of silence. Kevin and I stood up and shook hands.

"Give my best to your wife, Kevin. Hope it all works out."

"Yeah. Me too. Hope everything works out for you, too, Quay. Hope this trip produced good fruit."

"It has, my Brother."

I started to walk away when I heard him call out behind me:

"Hey, one more thing: pray for peace."

I just nodded and waved.

I sat near the front of the bus in contemplation.

Someone sat with me, but I didn't say anything. I just stared out the window. I stared out the window at the streets of Birmingham, teeming with people. Not blacks. Not whites. Not Hispanics. Not Jews.

Just people.

10

The days went quickly during my return visit to Tuscaloosa. It made a fantastic last destination and offered me an opportunity to tell about the places I had been since the last time I was in town. I got a perspective on where I had been and what things had happened to me both internally and externally.

I waited at the Tuscaloosa bus station for the last leg of my journey home. It was going to be a tough one; six hours east to Atlanta before even getting started north to Lancaster. It was warm and bright that day. I was standing outside the station basking in the sun wondering what was in store for me on this last ride. A young man waiting for a friend to arrive came over to talk.

"Where you headed, man?"

I paused for a moment. It was strange to comprehend what my answer was to be. The memories of bus stations throughout America flashed through my mind. Days and nights spent in bizarre places and under strange conditions came back to me, providing a feeling of being a survivalist. Scores of people to whom I would forever be indebted. The shell of a man who began this trip. A different man who was almost finished.

"Home . . . I'm headed home."

I boarded the bus for this final leg of the journey. Taking a spot in the front, I relaxed and went to sleep. Exhaustion was finally starting to set in from the late nights in Tuscaloosa, and the whole trip was finally catching up with me, too. It was good to be going home.

We arrived in Atlanta by the late afternoon. I had contemplated walking around the city during my two hour layover, but figured my best bet would be to get in line for the bus headed north. I was probably overly cautious, but having been successful most of the trip, the last thing I wanted to do was miss a bus because I wasn't in line. I was the first person waiting by the gate, but it wasn't long before others joined me.

It was going to be an interesting ride. There had been both a Harley-Davidson rally and Grateful Dead show that weekend, plus it was the beginning and end of spring break for different colleges.

The bikers were clad in their traditional garb: black leather, bandannas and chains. Standing behind them were about six wannabe hippies dressed in 60s throwback fashion; beads, multicolored hats, and baggy clothes. Interspersed were the college students with books and backpacks. And then there was myself, whatever I am.

The strange hodgepodge stood waiting for the bus to arrive. I spent time talking to a biker woman who was standing behind me, but people kept mainly to themselves and their small groups. I was encouraged because all I really wanted was an easy ride. No surprises. The better people got along in line, the more likely this would happen on the bus.

I was the first one to board the bus when it pulled into the station in Atlanta. I chose to sit in the aisle seat of row eight and watched as the rest of the riders boarded. There were about eight bikers and they took seats in the front. I was shocked as I thought they would be "back of the bus" types of people. Instead four young hippies came back, each one occupying his own pair of seats, all of them behind me. An attractive, young blond-haired girl took the seat directly in front of me. Two black guys boarded and took seats directly behind the bikers. All in all, the bus was at about half capacity, so there figured to be plenty of space for this strange array of characters.

I decided to start things off on the right foot with the girl in front of me.

"Hi. My name is Quay. With a Q. Where ya' headed'?"

She turned her beautiful blue eyes towards me and in a voice like a gentle whisper, "I'm headed to Charlotte. The name is

Marisa."

Marisa. How wonderful. This was one time that I wished the bus was full. I wished it was full and she wanted to sit next to me. I wished it was full, she wanted to sit next to me and I was good looking.

"Well, Marisa, I'm glad to meet you. I'm goin' to Pennsylvania, so I guess we'll be riding together for a while. I just . . ."

As I was finishing my sentence, I saw one more person arriving. One late entrant. One more fellow to add to the mix. He wasn't a tall man, but he had bulging muscles protruding from his all-black tee shirt. His arms were covered in tattoos. He looked a little bit like Burt Reynolds, but with a fu-manchu mustache and long, black hair flowing out from underneath his baseball hat. He wore skin-tight jeans, cowboy boots, and a scowl.

He walked silently down the aisle to the very last seat, giving some nods along the way as if to say, "I have arrived. Don't #!@*& with me." He sat down and pulled out a fifth of vodka and said to the hippies, "It's a long ride boys. Better settle in and work on gettin' some #!@*&."

Stunned back into the conversation, Marisa encouraged me, "You just what, Clay?"

"Uh, it's Quay. Forget it."

I sat quietly, as did everybody, occasionally looking back at Vodka Guy to see what he was doing. He seemed content and was keeping to himself so I thought I was making too much out of it. I just couldn't believe he wasn't being discreet. Drinking alcohol on the Greyhound carried a $300 fine and a night in jail, but I guess Vodka Guy figured no one would rat on him if he offered a little to everyone. To be honest, he really wasn't too bad other than his foul language. I had heard so many swear words on this trip though, it didn't bother me much. There hadn't been any problems, but I felt there was something not quite right about him.

Vodka guy tired of trying to talk to the hippies and he

stumbled past me with two paper cups holding a shot of booze in each. One hippie said to the one closest to the back,

"How much has he had to drink so far?"

The other one peeked ever so slowly over the seat and whispered, "About half the bottle."

We had only been traveling an hour and this guy had already drank a lot of alcohol. He was taking the cups up to one of the biker ladies to offer her a cocktail. He certainly was smooth.

Vodka Guy sat down with the lucky biker lady, leaving the back seat unoccupied. He had moved his bag and bottle into another seat, therefore giving the impression he was no longer sitting in the back seat. The two black guys near the front of the bus decided, for whatever reason, to move into Vodka guy's now unoccupied seat. I wasn't sure if this was a breach of bus etiquette or not. It seemed that moving your things meant you were no longer sitting there, but I wasn't sure if Vodka Guy assumed it was his seat for the rest of the trip or what.

Vodka Guy flirted for about ten minutes longer, but apparently wasn't having any luck. He began to take the long walk back the aisle, swaying with the gentle whoosh of the bus. I could tell he was starting to feel the alcohol. When he arrived at his old seat, like Baby Bear to Goldilocks, he was shocked to find someone in it.

"Oh, no you don't. Oh, no you don't!" He sputtered. "You guys ain't takin' my seat!"

"Sorry, bro," and the two young black men got up and casually walked back to the front of the bus and sat down.

Vodka Guy wanted a confrontation though. He marched right up and started to whisper something into the one black guy's ear.

Suddenly, the black guy stood up and started shoving Vodka Guy to the back.

"Just sit down! Just sit the #!@*& down."

As he pushed him, Vodka Guy would fall into the seats,

sometimes right on top of the person sitting there. One of these people was Marisa. Now I was getting mad. That was my girlfriend! (She just didn't know it.) Like all great heroes though, I just let the two go by and offered my empty seat to Marisa and she obliged. Who says I needed a full bus to get a beautiful woman to sit with me? All I needed was one drunk buffoon.

When the black guy finally got Vodka Guy to the back seat, he gave him a swift smack upside the head and growled, "Just stay the #!@*& back here!"

The hippies and I stared in disbelief as the black guy headed back to his seat. I was amazed for a couple of reasons. One, it was the first confrontation I had seen on the bus where there was physical contact. Two, the bus driver hadn't heard or seen anything that had just gone on. Granted, he was busy driving, but in most my trips the bus drivers seemed to have an eye on what was happening. I don't think he was ignoring it. I think he just missed it. Not to be lost in all the action was the fact that young Marisa had come to me for comfort. That was probably the most amazing part.

I thought that Vodka Guy had either passed out or the black guy had knocked him out because he was lying there with his eyes closed. I was hoping that he was out for the night, not just for our sake, but his own. Causing trouble seemed to be on his mind.

I hoped I could spend some time getting to know Marisa better, but our discussion was interrupted by the awakening of Vodka Guy. He was groggy either from the alcohol, the sleep, or the smack to the head. Probably a combination. Within two minutes of waking, he was drinking again.

After taking a couple hits off the bottle, he arose and started making his rounds. It was now well into night, so the bus was dark. When it got dark it usually signaled sleep, and that's what the hippies were doing. I had stayed awake to see what Vodka Guy was going to do next.

He walked up to the hippie closest to the back.

"Heeeeyyy . . . Buuuudddyy!" His speech was slow and slurred. He stood there swaying, but the hippie continued to sleep. Maybe the hippie thought it was one of his friends. Maybe he was a heavy sleeper. Whatever the case, he was lying there with his eyes closed.

Vodka Guy reached down and poked him. The hippie sat up, not knowing what was going on. He looked to see that it was Vodka guy and he said, "What the #!@*& do you want?!!"

Vodka guy had a big grin and was kept saying "Hey! I've got something for you."

The hippie yelled back, "Just leave me the #!@*& alone!"

In his slurred speech, Vodka guy said, "But I have something for you," and proceeded to push his obscenity to the extreme.

"Get the #!@*& away from me, you freak!" the hippie shouted, as he scrambled to get as close to the window and as far away as possible.

Luckily it was dark and hard to see, but his actions were disturbing. Vodka Guy was making his way to each of the four hippies, mumbling in gibberish. I decided that I had had enough. If Vodka guy tried to pull that with Marisa and me, I was going to lay him out. I waited. He was getting closer and closer, and I made a fist ready to punch him in the face or in the groin, whichever was closer. The bus started slowing down, though, and we pulled into a stop in South Carolina. Vodka Guy went to his seat and sat down.

Vodka Guy stayed on the bus while the rest of us stood outside the terminal complaining about him.

"That dude is sick, man. Sick!" said one hippie.

"Yeah, he's all #!@*& up!"

Most of the riders conversed about the way the trip was going and how one drunk moron was ruining it. For all our complaining though, no one did anything. Vodka Guy stayed on the bus, and I hoped that he had passed out. I'll give him credit. I never saw someone drink so much so quickly and not pass out by this point.

We slowly boarded the bus again and everyone went back to the seat they had occupied. We picked up some new riders at the South Carolina station, two young black men in their early twenties. The two new riders sat directly in front of Vodka Guy.

"Whash up . . . fellas?" Vodka Guy had taken on the role as welcome wagon for this bus and wanted to get acquainted with our new friends.

"Nothin', buddy. Nothin'." The one New Rider said, laughing as he did so.

"Howsh it goin'. . . .pals?"

"What's wrong with this guy? Is he #!@*& up?" questioned New Rider 1.

One of the hippies responded, "Yeah, dude. He's all #!@*& up. He drank almost a whole #!@*& bottle of vodka since Atlanta!"

The two new riders looked at each other and busted out laughing. None of us told the new guys about Vodka Guy's "exhibition" though, as we figured he would let them know what he was all about soon enough. Vodka Guy continued to try and carry on a conversation, but the new riders soon tired of his antics and chose to ignore him.

Vodka Guy started to feel slighted. He wasn't getting attention anymore. To make his presence known once again, he began to flick the ear of New Rider 1.

New Rider 1 wheeled around hard.

"What the #!@*& are you doin', you #!@*&! I'll come back there and kick your #!@*&!"

The air was thick. The tension was unbelievable. There was silence except for the hum of the bus, and Vodka guy muttering, "#!@*& you."

New Rider 1 had turned forward, and I quickly turned too, not wanting to piss either of them off by being nosy. But I had my eye on the back of the bus. It was dark, but I didn't want to miss what was happening. I stole a glance back and saw the bony fingers in position again.

Flick.

This time New Rider 1 jumped out of his seat and on top of Vodka Guy, whacking him hard, twice right across the side of the head. "I told you not to touch me, mother#!@*&! I told you!" He let loose with another crack across Vodka Guy's face.

By this time New Rider 2 was also piled on top of Vodka Guy. "Are you #!@*& crazy, man? All #!@*& up and flickin' a brother's ear? He'll #!@*& you up real bad, man? Know what I mean?"

Vodka Guy wasn't hearing any of it as he was trying to catch his breath from the weight crushing him.

The New Riders moved back to their seats and tried to calm down. I was sitting in astonishment that the bus driver still hadn't heard anything that was going on, especially with how loud those slaps to the head were. Marisa must have been a pretty tough girl. She was less scared than I was.

"Serves him right, the stupid #!@*&," she decried.

All I wanted was an easy ride home and this was not it. I was mad at Vodka Guy myself. He was not playing by bus rules. He was in violation of bus etiquette on many fronts. The infrastructure of respect, understanding, and patience was being broken by his unbridled ignorance.

And then it hit me.

His behavior was the perfect symbol of my racism. I had spent my whole life treating people different than me like second class citizens. I had no respect, understanding, or patience for anyone who wasn't doing what I was doing or believing what I was believing. It is often said, "What can one person do?" yet here was a perfect example of what could happen. One person can easily make a big impact on society. Easily. And that doesn't mean in only a bad way. One good example speaks volumes just as one bad example can ruin everything.

I had broken my life down into a community of 47, the greatest number of people who were on any particular bus at any particular time. I had realized that each person made a difference in the community of the bus. Being such a small group, it really brought to light how wrong I was in my feelings for blacks and other minorities. It did make a difference.

I then transferred that on a larger scale to the overall community I lived in. I had never questioned my racism, and I never believed it made a difference. I realized now that it did. My racism was like the drunken antics of Vodka Guy. Some may find it funny; some may not care at all; some may even turn the other way. The prospect of a respectable community, though, was being ruined because I was too dumb to see that what it took was inside of me. To build a respectable community, I had to be a respectable part of it. That was something I had complete control over.

As I pondered my personal changes, the situation worsened on the bus.

Vodka Guy was beyond help at this point. He had no idea what he was doing or how destructive it was to the bus community or himself. He reached forward one last time and flicked New Rider 1's ear.

This time though, New Rider 1 didn't flip out. He didn't yell. He didn't jump into the back seat and start wailing on Vodka Guy. No, not this time.

This time he pulled out a knife.

He didn't show it to anybody other than New Rider 2, but I could see it. He was gripping the handle tightly as he rested it on his leg. He wasn't threatening Vodka Guy with it, but I assumed that was his next move.

Like a blessing from above, we pulled into a scheduled stop at this time. The driver called out, "Okay, folks. We have a fifteen minute stop to refuel. Why doesn't everybody get a drink or something." I knew somebody who had more than enough to drink.

Everyone got off to get some air. Everybody except Vodka Guy. As I stood on the sidewalk, to my left I overheard New Rider 1 tell New Rider 2, "I'm just goin' to get rerouted. I don't #!@*& need this, you know what I mean? #!@*& that. There's gonna' be trouble."

New Rider 2 understood but decided to continue the trip. To my right I heard some of the other passengers gathered in a cluster and complaining.

"He's ruining the trip for everybody!" exclaimed one older lady.

"He's just repulsive. It's impossible for me to sleep knowing he's wandering around the bus all drunk and everything." chimed in another.

"He's, like, out there, man. Polluted."

One guy had changed his ticket. A number of people had finally moved to different seats on the bus. Everyone seemed to have a complaint about not being able to relax out of fear. It seemed ridiculous to me that we all stood around complaining about the guy, when there seemed to be an easy solution.

Frustrated, I said, "Why don't we just tell the bus driver?"

Everyone looked at one another waiting for someone to volunteer. I said, "What's the matter?"

"What if he gets pissed and goes after the one who reported him?"came the response from one of the bikers. I had met a lot of bikers in my life. I had never met one afraid of *anything*, and these men were scared of one drunk fool?

I finally said, "Look, I don't care. I'll tell him, but I would appreciate if you all came along to verify my story."

The cowards nodded in agreement and I marched over to the bus driver with a group of ten or so following closely behind, somewhat like a bus-riding Moses.

"Sir, there's an extremely drunk guy on the bus and he's making everyone uncomfortable. He's just wreaking havoc."

The bus driver looked astonished.

"This is happening on my bus?"

"Yes, sir. Yes it is." Behind me the people were either nodding their heads or saying "yes."

"Where is he now?" the driver questioned.

"He's still on the bus . . . sitting in the very back seat. You can't miss him."

The driver immediately hopped on and we heard him yelling. "How dare you get drunk on my bus! Get the #!@*& up, right now! Get your sorry #!@*& off of my bus!"

He marched Vodka Guy up the aisle and off the bus to where we were standing. We were quickly ordered to get back on.

We sat staring out the window as Vodka Guy took yet another slug off the bottle. That was about all that was left. None of us said anything as we watched the police car pull up, cuff him, and take him away.

I started to feel like a rat. If I could have put up with him a little longer, he wouldn't have been arrested. Maybe I was in the wrong. But my feelings changed when I received a couple handshakes from the riders and several said, "Thanks." New Rider 2 gave me a thumbs up, and Marisa, well Marisa didn't say much other than moving back into her original seat.

I felt less like a rat when I realized that I had been the voice of the bus majority. Sometimes taking a stand will require the courage to do things other people won't. I represented the way we felt and wasn't afraid to take action to do something about it. Maybe it even helped Vodka guy. A night in jail may have caused him to think about his life and what he was going to do with it.

We traveled into the night and reached Charlotte somewhere around 1:00 a.m.

"See you, Marisa. It's been some ride."

I gave her that patented country boy smile and extended my arms for a well deserved hug. We had been through so much together.

"Yeah. Take it easy, Clay," she said during our short, weak embrace.

As people boarded in Charlotte, I was lucky enough to retain my own own seat. All I wanted to do was sleep. I got into my patented sleeper position and drifted off into dreamland.

We hadn't gotten far when a lady in the back started screaming, "Stop the bus! Stop the bus!"

"What now?!" I thought.

The driver came to an abrupt halt and started shouting orders, "See what her problem is!" He was rushing back the aisle and all heads had turned to see who she was and what was going on. When the driver got back to her seat, he breathlessly said,

"What's the problem?!"

"My baby is throwing up all over me!"

Now, correct me if I'm wrong, but isn't that what babies do?

The furious driver spoke slowly and angrily, but without shouting. "Lady, don't you ever holler 'Stop the bus!' again for something like that. Even if your baby craps in his diaper!"

We all chuckled at his sarcasm.

A number of people helped get her cleaned up and calmed down, and I found myself to be indifferent to the whole situation. It wasn't that I wasn't sympathetic, it was just a mild moment in the travels I had experienced. I had been on smoking buses and through cancellations, watched a guy pull a knife out, and encountered just about every type of individual imaginable. And now I had seen a lady with vomit all over her chest. There wasn't much left to surprise me. I liked that feeling of completeness.

It was still dark outside when we arrived in Richmond, and I was amazed to find the line so long for the bus to Baltimore. Standing directly in front of me was a girl about nineteen, and she was having trouble reading her ticket. I sensed a little bus anxiety. Being the seasoned veteran I was, plus recognizing any good time to flirt, I offered to help.

"Do you need any help?"

"I'm just not sure this is the right line or not. I've never ridden the bus before and I have no clue what's going on."

"Here. Let me look at it . . . Oh, you're going to York. I'm headed that way. Just follow me."

She smiled, not exactly sure if this was a good or bad thing for her.

As we stood in line, I started to make small talk with my new friend from York. The throw up lady came over to us, and interrupted our conversation.

"Just look at my shirt. It's all covered with puke and it really stinks. Just look at it!"

I looked, and not having any clue why she was showing it to us, I stated, "Yes. I see that."

Then she walked away.

Weird.

We boarded the bus headed to Baltimore, and the York girl sat with me. Since I hardly slept a lick the night before, I didn't even try to impress her with everything I had done the last couple of months. I just fell asleep.

When we arrived in Baltimore, our driver told us that we should be leaving from gate number three. Both the York girl and I would be taking the northern bus, with her getting off in York, while I would be taking it the whole way to Harrisburg where I would pick up my last bus to Lancaster.

Something didn't seem right as we stood in line though. We were the only ones in it and I was sure that it was time to board. I took a second to examine the electronic arrival/departure screen and realized we were leaving from gate two, and the bus was already loading. I grabbed my friend and said, "Come on!" We ran and jumped on, and I yanked my bag through the doors just as the driver pulled them closed.

I found it to be another representation of where I had been and where I was. It took me back to my first bus switch in D.C.

when Slick so graciously offered his help. When I looked at that screen the first time, I had no clue what it meant. For as much as Slick bothered me, he put me on the right path. Now I was using my acquired skills to help someone else. I was passing on my knowledge so someday she, too, could pass it on. The bus society was about learning and sharing, and that's why I loved it so much.

We traveled north to York, and I watched as my friend got off and waved to me through the window.

We arrived in Harrisburg an hour later. I could have waited five hours to catch a bus to Lancaster, but I was too excited to get started on my new life back home. My mom and sister made the the forty-five minute drive to Harrisburg to pick me up.

Mom came into the station to find me. I was seated on a bench, unshaven, disheveled, and smelling badly. I saw a look in her eyes like, "I can't believe you made it, but I'm glad you did." As often as we complain about our parents, there is nothing like their reassurance to give us peace.

As we made our way out of the station, I was leading the way. I saw a man walking towards us. When he got within speaking distance he said, "Whaddya' need?" I had learned in my travels that this is a drug dealing technique. He assumed I was looking for drugs and was asking what type I needed.

The easiest way to get rid of a drug dealer is to be polite, but firm.

"Nothing. I'm good."

As we got to the car, Mom said, "What was that all about?"

"Oh, nothing," I replied.

In that moment, I realized I had seen and experienced more in my nine weeks than most people will in a lifetime. I began to understand the weight of the trip and the changes in my life. I thought the journey was ending, but it had just begun.

I left Strasburg to see what America was really like. Learning about America, though, taught me about myself. Who I am and who I am becoming will never cease until I am in my grave. Just as I challenged myself on this trip, I will need to continue challenging myself at every phase of life if I want to make the most of it. For now, though, I had come home a successful traveler. A wiser individual. A new man.

And the adventure continues. . .

Conclusion

After arriving home, I was amazed at how nothing had changed. My mom's hair was still the same. There were no new buildings in Strasburg. My friends and family were still going through their daily lives just as they had always done. I don't know why I expected things to be different. I guess you figure that when you've changed, lots of other stuff changes, too. But it doesn't.

I think that is the hardest part about returning from a journey. You aren't the same, but everything else is. I've been to all fifty states, twenty-seven countries, and five continents and coming home has always been difficult. You only have three choices: Move somewhere else, go back to the way you've always done things, or begin to act as a new person in the old surroundings. I've always chosen to stay where I am, but do things differently. It's expensive, though. It has cost me friends. It has cost me respect. It has cost me acceptance. Things cannot and will not be the same. Change comes with a price, and it is heavy. But to have seen the truth and pass it by is unacceptable. I cannot live that way.

What I learned on this trip was much deeper than simply addressing my racism. In fact, I would go as far as saying that confronting my prejudice wasn't what I really learned. Prejudice was the first lens through which I began to challenge and discern my beliefs. I found that I was deficient in many, many ways, mentally, physically, morally, and spiritually. Too many people consider this simply a story about a man changing his views on race. That's true on the surface. There is so much more, though.

In contemporary society, it seems most people want to be victims. People sue tobacco manufacturers because they get lung cancer. Overweight people sue McDonald's because they have heart problems. Today's youth are labeled ADD, when it used to be called "disrespectful." We have turned our personal challenges into blame for everything and everybody other than ourselves. We accept no responsibility. The reason I hate racism is that it makes victims out of everybody. Some people have a better reason than others to feel victimized, but when do we get past that point and accept responsibility for our lives?

On the bus, I finally took responsibility for my words, actions, and beliefs. I finally realized that my miserable state of existence had nothing to do with blacks, Latinos, Jews, government, parents, friends, upbringing, or education. It was my own doing and I wanted to change it.

How does this happen, though? How does one suddenly begin to look at his life differently? What made my time on the bus any different than any other point in my life? I titled my book *Revelation of a Redneck* for a reason. A revelation is hard to explain. In fact, a revelation implies that something supernatural is at work. There needs to be One who is doing the revealing. I wondered, "Could this be God?"

This revelation weighed heavily on my soul year after year, forcing me to examine many other characteristics of my life. I was being broken down on a daily basis and was opened to see how corrupt my heart had been all along. A culmination of events led me to sobriety on July 12, 1995 and caused me to dig even deeper into what was really revealed on the bus several years prior.

I had once heard that any attempt to study Christianity must begin with the empty tomb of Jesus Christ. This man from history predicted that His tomb would be empty three days after being placed in it. And it was. I decided to start here.

I researched and studied all that I could about this man who claimed to be God. In His teachings, Jesus said He was the fulfillment of the Old Testament prophesies in Isaiah about a "suffering servant." He claimed to be the Son of God, and many in His time believed. He also prophesied that He would die for the sins of the elect, and that three days later He would be raised from the dead to sit at the right hand of the Father in heaven. By Christ's work, I could have my corrupt heart made pure; the only way to the Father was through Him. It sounded outrageous.

Yet, as I engrossed myself in a study of this man, there was one thing both sacred and secular historical texts agreed upon: the tomb where they buried Jesus was empty three days after He was placed inside. It was a factual event from history.

Of course, the next logical question would be, "What happened to the body?" I explored the possibility that it was stolen. I researched the reasoning that Jesus wasn't really dead. I tried to write this off as a mythical story about a good guy named Jesus who lived in the first century, and that these myths were invented to pass along to the next generation. None of the answers worked, though, except one. Jesus was who He said He was, the Son of God.

I read further into the Bible, and learned in Romans 10:9 "that if you confess with your mouth Jesus as Lord, and believe in your heart that God raised Him from the dead, you shall be saved." I believed it. I believed it with all my heart, mind, soul and strength. And I confessed it. Jesus Christ is the Son of God, sent to earth to pay the price of my guilt as a sinner.

I realized that it *was* God all along, beginning with the revelation on the bus, and culminating in that moment by granting me the faith to believe. By His mercy and grace, I was given eternal life.

Regardless of where you are in your walk of life, I urge you to explore this man from history named Jesus. You must study His claims before considering him a "good man" or a "prophet." You must answer some questions about Him before dismissing Him as a mythical figure or just plain crazy. I encourage you to do so with an open mind, praying that God will reveal the truth to you.

Thanks for listening to my story and reading all the way to the last page. You have a story, too. I encourage you to ask yourself the question, "How will it end?"